Joseph Pergmayr

The Truths of Salvation

Joseph Pergmayr

The Truths of Salvation

ISBN/EAN: 9783744659673

Printed in Europe, USA, Canada, Australia, Japan

Cover: Foto ©Lupo / pixelio.de

More available books at **www.hansebooks.com**

TRUTHS OF SALVATION.

BY

REV. J. PERGMAYR, S. J.,

Translated from the German by a Father of the same Society,

With the Permission of Superiors.

"Learn, for the sake of thy Creator, to overcome thyself in all things: and then thou shalt be able to attain divine knowledge."—
FOLLOWING OF CHRIST, III BOOK, 42 Chapter.

NEW YORK, CINCINNATI, AND ST. LOUIS:
BENZIGER BROTHERS,
Publishers to the Holy Apostolic See.
1882.

Imprimatur.

JOHN, CARDINAL MCCLOSKEY,
Archbishop of New York.

Copyright, 1882, by BENZIGER BROTHERS.

Newark, N. J., February 15, 1882.

REV. DEAR FATHER:

I take great pleasure in recommending Pergmayr's "Truths of Salvation," which you have had the happy inspiration to translate from the German into English. The work itself is one of great merit, and calculated to do much good, and to be a safe and efficient guide to souls aspiring to Christian perfection.

Hoping that the book in its English dress will meet with all the success it so richly deserves, I remain

your Servant in Christ,

✠ W. M. WIGGER,
Bishop of Newark.

PREFACE.

THERE are few who reap permanent fruit from a retreat. The cause is twofold. First, during this time they do not enter seriously into a thorough consideration of the eternal truths. These truths being only superficially reflected on, exert, consequently, but little influence upon their lives. Secondly, they do not fully examine the state of their souls, and therefore not knowing their defects leave them uncorrected. Self-knowledge is the first step to amendment of life. Father Lallemant, in "The Spiritual Doctrine," says: "The heart recoils from nothing so much as this search and scrutiny which make it see and feel its own miseries. All the powers of our soul are disordered beyond measure, and this we do not wish to know, because the knowledge is humiliating to us. Our soul does not enter into itself except with pain, seeing nothing but sins, miseries, and confusion. So that, to avoid this distressing and humiliating sight, it hurries instantly out again, and goes to seek its consolation in creatures, unless we keep it carefully to its duty." In the "Lives of the Saints," the Rev. Dr. Alban Butler remarks: "A true penitent must apply himself to the difficult work of self-examination in order to discover every latent inordinate affection or passion. Sin must be pursued home to its roots, and the evil tendencies of the soul dislodged thence, otherwise all will be to no purpose. By earnest prayer, mortification, alms, and holy meditation, penitential sorrow must be improved till it has forced its way into the innermost recesses of the soul, shaken all the powers of sin, and formed the new man, so little understood among Christians, though it is the very essence of a Christian life."

The present little work is offered to those who earnestly desire to consider the truths of salvation and to acquire self-knowledge. They must, however, bear in mind, that the thorough consideration of divine things and of themselves must be their own work and not that of others. It rests with themselves to elicit particular resolutions and affections. St. Ignatius says: "Should one happen to discover, whether through his own reasoning or through a light from heaven, anything which helps, in the least degree, to throw light on the subject, he derives from this a far more pleasant relish and much richer fruit than from the fuller statement and explanation of another. For it is not the quantity of knowledge, but the internal perception and relish of the objects of knowledge which satisfy the desires of the soul."

But some are unaccustomed to meditate; others are incapable, from weakness or indisposition, of mental application: both classes will be aided by this little work. They should read, however, the meditations and self-examinations very slowly so as to be able to evolve from their own minds the affections they see suggested therein. Those who wish to use with advantage "The Truths of Salvation" must peruse them often after the retreat, till they have so far imbibed them that their lives may be modelled thereon.

The success of a retreat must be attributed to

grace more than to our own efforts: "Thou wilt never attain to this unless thou be prevented and drawn by His grace, that so thou mayest be united to Him alone, when thou hast cast out and dismissed all others." (Following of Christ, i. 8. 5.)

If we would become fit instruments in the hands of God, we could perform wonders. This retreat, though limited to eight days, contains the four weeks of the spiritual exercises in an abridged form. To have a full knowledge of these four weeks, let us hear **the words of his Eminence, Cardinal Wiseman:**

"The reader will observe that the Exercises are divided into four weeks; and each of these has a specific object to advance the exercitant an additional step towards perfect virtue. If the work of each week be thoroughly done, this is actually accomplished.

"The first week has for its aim the cleansing of the conscience from past sin and of the affections from their future dangers. For this purpose, the soul is made to convince itself deeply of the true end of its being—to serve God and be saved; and of the real worth of all else. This consideration has been justly called by St. Ignatius, the principle or foundation of the entire system.

"No limits are put to the time that may be spent upon this subject; it ought not to be left till the mind is made up that nothing is worth aiming at but God and salvation, and that to all other things we must be indifferent. They are but instruments or hindrances in the acquisition of these, and accordingly they must be treated. It is clear that the person, who has brought himself to this state of mind, has fully prepared himself for submitting to whatever he may be required to do by God for attaining his end.

"Upon this groundwork is raised the duty of the first week. Considerations of the punishment of sin which lead us gradually to an abhorrence of it in itself, make the sinner sift and thoroughly unburden his conscience. The fear of God, which is the beginning of wisdom, is thus the first agent in the great work of change; a change not prospective or mental, but real. Sin is abandoned, hated, loathed.

"At the conclusion of the painful task, the soul finds itself prostrate and full of anxieties. The past is remedied; but what is to be done for the future? A rule to guide us, an example to encourage us, high motives to animate us, are now wanting; and the three following weeks secure us these.

"In the second, the life of Christ is made our model. By a series of contemplations of it we become familiar with His virtues, enamored of His perfections; we learn, by copying Him, to be obedient to God and man, meek, humble, affectionate, zealous, charitable, forgiving; men of only one wish and one thought—that of doing ever God's holy will alone, discreet, devout, observant of every law, scrupulous performers of every duty. Every meditation on these subjects shows us how to do all this—in fact, makes us really do it.

"Still, up to this point we have been dealt with kindly, as the Apostles were treated by their good Master. He told them not of these things—that is, of His sufferings—at first, lest sorrow should fill their hearts (John xvi. 5, 6). The milk of consolation and encouragement must precede the strong food of patience and conformity. The third week brings us to this. Having desired and tried to be like Christ in action, we are brought to wish and endeavor to be like unto Him in suffering. For this purpose His sacred Passion becomes the engrossing subject of the Exercises. The soul which has been brought near Him in admiration now clings to Him in loving sympathy—nay, finds her admiration redoubled at His divine bearing in sorrow, ignominy, and pain. Having already made up her mind to be like Him in all things, she is not now to be scared from resemblance by the bitterness of suffering or disgrace. On the contrary, she wishes to suffer for Him, for the very love's sake, which made Him so suffer. Every meditation on the Passion strengthens, deepens, matures this feeling, and renders it a new power and affection of the soul. She has become a martyr in resolution and desire; she would go forth from this holy work of meditation to the realization of her earnest desire to suffer with Jesus. She is prepared for mortifications, for tribulations, persecutions, for death, for anything whereby she may be likened to her Lord and God.

" But she must be convinced and feel that if she suffers, she shall also be glorified with Him; and hence the fourth and concluding week raises the soul to the consideration of those glories which crowned the humiliations and sufferings of our Lord. As throughout He is represented to us in His blessed Humanity as being our model, so here are our thoughts directed to Him, triumphant over death, but still conversing among men—those now who love Him, that so our love may be likewise with Him, in holy conversation and familiar intercourse, and so He may draw up our hearts with Him when He ascends to His Father; and there they may ever abide where our treasure is. Thus have we been gradually raised from fear to love, which henceforward is the 'informing principle' (to borrow a phrase from the Schools) of our lives and being.

"It is clear that if these various principles and feelings have been really infused into us, if they have been worked into our hearts, so as to form a part of their real practical influences, we shall come from the Exercises, duly performed, completely changed, and fitted for our future course. Many indeed have experienced this. They have entered the place appointed for them, like a vessel shattered by the storms, bruised, and crippled, and useless; they have come forth with every breach repaired, every disfigurement removed; and what is of more importance, furnished with rudder and compass, sails and anchor, all that can direct and guide, impel and secure them. What wonder if their songs of gratitude and joy resound along the main?

"It will be seen that the Weeks of the Exercises do not mean necessarily a period of seven days. The original duration of their performance was certainly a month; but, even so, more or less time was allotted to each week's work, according to the discretion of the Director. Now, except in very particular circumstances, the entire period is abridged to ten days; sometimes it is still further reduced. But even so the form and distribution of the Exercises must be strictly kept, and no anticipations or inversions must be permitted. It is impossible to make the slightest change in this respect without injury.

"What has been said will perhaps explain, though inadequately, the wonderful power and efficacy of the 'Spiritual Exercises of St. Ignatius' in thoroughly reforming the soul, and bringing it from sin to steady virtue. But the grand secret may be said to consist in two points:

"First, the entire work is performed by principles, not by emotions which pass away. Conviction of the truth and reality of all that is inculcated is aimed at and secured; reason is enlisted on the side of conscience, and whatever use is made of the feelings in the course of the Exercises, is but as scaffolding to assist in the erection of a solid structure of virtue, which will stand and weather the storm after it has been removed.

"Secondly, the mind is made to act throughout, and to work out its own resolutions. Nothing is imposed on us by others, either through persuasion or by authority; we are made to think, to conclude, to determine, and to act by a process essentially our own, so that there is no escape, and no danger from the reaction of self-love. No influence has been used, further than to guide rightly the exercise of our own powers; and even that direction has been given to us with our eyes open, and under the full conviction that we cannot shrink from a single step without going against reason and conscience."

Father Joseph Pergmayr, the author of "The Truths of Salvation," was born in Bavaria in 1713; in 1733 he entered the Society of Jesus. This holy man preached during many years at Munich, and guided several religious communities in the path of perfection. Being palsied in his hands he was obliged to use them both in order to write legibly; he was the author of various pious works full of the unction of the Holy Ghost. He died a holy death at Munich on the 23d of March, 1765. The "Truths of Salvation" will be found very useful to all Religious, but lay-persons desirous of laboring at their salvation will not find them less profitable.

May this little work contribute to the greater glory of God and to the salvation and perfection of souls!

In your charity pray for the

TRANSLATOR.

CONTENTS.

	PAGE
PREFACE	3

FIRST DAY.

The groundwork of the retreat ... 21

Meditation I.—The End of Man.

POINT I.

It is just to live conformably to your end ... 21
Affections.—Confession. Contrition ... 23

POINT II.

It is advantageous to live conformably to your end ... 24
Affections.—Hope. Contempt of all temporal things ... 25

POINT III.

It is necessary to live conformably to your end ... 26
Affections.—Fear. Resolution. A prayer to implore Divine grace ... 27

Meditation II.—The End of Religious.

POINT I.

The excellence of your state requires of you to live conformably to your end ... 29
Affections.—Esteem for religious Vocation. An act of self-abasement ... 31

POINT II.

The extraordinary love of God for you, requires of you to live according to your end ... 32
Affections.—Gratitude. An act of self-abasement ... 33

POINT III.

It is absolutely necessary for you to live according to your end.. 34
Affections.—Fear. Resolution. Love.................. 36

Meditation III.—On complete indifference towards creatures.

POINT I.

God's supreme dominion requires of you to keep yourself in a state of perfect indifference.................. 38
Affections.—Acknowledgment of the dominion of God. Sorrow and Contrition............................ 39

POINT II.

The Providence of God requires of you to keep yourself in complete indifference....................... 40
Affections.—Confidence. Self-abasement............. 42

POINT III.

The justice of God requires of you to keep yourself in complete indifference............................ 43
Affections.—Act of Humility. Resolution. A prayer to implore grace................................... 44

FIRST WEEK.—THE PURGATIVE WAY.

SECOND DAY.

Meditation I.—On the sin of the rebel angels and that of our first parents.

POINT I.

The punishment of the rebel angels shows what an infinite evil sin is.................................... 46
Affections.—Admiration. Contrition................. 48

POINT II.

The punishment of our first parents also shows the infinite evil of sin.................................... 49
Affections.—Fear. Contrition........................ 51

POINT III.

Reflections which necessarily follow the consideration of these truths.................................... 52
Affections.—Compunction. Thanksgiving. Supplication. 53

Meditation II.—On actual or personal sins.

POINT I.

We may judge of the infinite malice of sin from its effects.................................... 55
Affections.—Confusion. A prayer to implore grace.... 57

POINT II.

We also learn the infinite malice of sin from the abject state of one who offends God.................... 58
Affections.—Self-abasement. Compunction.......... 60

POINT III.

The Supreme Majesty of God who is offended, plainly shows what an infinite evil sin is................. 61
Affections.—Self-accusation. Compunction.......... 62

Meditation III.—On the first pain of Hell— The pain of loss.

POINT I.

The damned in Hell lose God, their sovereign good and their supreme happiness...................... 64
Affections.—Confession. Resolution................. 66

POINT II.

The damned have in God their greatest enemy........ 67
Affections.—Fear. Compunction. Resolution........ 68

THIRD DAY.

Meditation IV.—On the second pain of Hell—The pain of the senses.

POINT I.
	PAGE
The pains of the senses in Hell are terrible in their nature..	70
Affections.—Fear. A prayer for grace.................	71

POINT II.
The pains of the senses in Hell are terrible in their duration...	72
Affections.—Thanksgiving. Compunction............	74

Meditation V.—What fruits shall now be gathered from the preceding meditations?

FIRST FRUIT.
To conceive a thorough sorrow for our sins...........	75

SECOND FRUIT.
To satisfy as much as possible the Divine Justice for past sins...	76

THIRD FRUIT.
To avoid all venial sins, especially those which lead to mortal sin..	77

SECOND WEEK.—THE ILLUMINATIVE WAY.

Meditation I.—On the reign of Christ.

POINT I.
It is just to follow Christ...........................	80
Affections.—Thanksgiving. Resolution...............	81

POINT II.
It is easy to follow Christ..........................	82
Affections.—Hope and Confidence...................	84

POINT III.

It is necessary to follow Christ.................. 85
Affections.—Compunction. An act of Self-offering.... 86

FOURTH DAY.

Meditation II.—On the wonderful humility which Christ exhibited in His Incarnation and His Birth.

POINT I.

Christ in His Incarnation and Birth utterly debased
  Himself.. 88
Affections.—Confusion. Compunction............... 90

POINT II.

Christ from His birth out, all through life, willingly
  submitted to all the humiliations which came upon
  Him from others............................... 91
Affections.—Contempt of one's self. Acknowledgment. 92

POINT III.

Considerations on the humility of Jesus Christ........ 93
Affections.—Confession and Sorrow. Resolutions and
  Supplication.................................... 94

Meditation III.—On the wonderful obedience of Christ in His hidden life.

POINT I.

Jesus underwent for the love of His Heavenly Father
  and for me all the hardships which perfect obedience
  invariably brings on............................ 96
Affections.—Self-abasement. Compunction.......... 98

POINT II.

On the wonderful happiness of a soul that practises
  blind and therefore perfect obedience............. 99
Affections.—Faith. Hope and confidence. An act of
  love and self-offering.... 101

Meditation IV.—On the wonderful charity and meekness of Christ in His public life.

POINT I. PAGE

Christ underwent first the hardships which render charity and meekness difficult.................. 103
Affections.—Confusion. Resolution.................. 105

POINT II.

The marvellous qualities of Jesus' charity for us....... 106
Affections.—Compunction. Love. Resolution........ 107

FIFTH DAY.

Meditation V.—The conclusion of the Second Week. Maxims of spiritual life.

Exercises of Obedience, of Humility, of Meekness, and Charity 111

THIRD WEEK.

Intermediate Meditation I.—The Two Standards.

POINT I.

Whom we are to follow—Jesus Christ or Satan—may be seen from the design of the two leaders whom we now propose................ 113
Affections... 115

POINT II.

Whom we are to follow—Jesus Christ or Satan—may be seen by the ends to which both lead.............. 115
Affections 117

POINT III.

Whom we are to follow—Jesus or Satan—may be seen by the end for which God has called us to the religious life 118
Affections.—Faith. Desire of union with God........ 120

Intermediate Meditation II.—The three classes of men.

POINT I.

To the first class belong those who aim at perfection, but only in desire; they speak of it continually, but do not wish it sincerely.................... 121
Affections.—Fear. Compunction... 123

POINT II.

To the second class belong those who wish, it is true, to aim at perfection, but have not a universal and generous will 124
Affections.—Acknowledgment. Resolution.......... 126

POINT III.

To the third class belong those who have an earnest and generous wish to arrive at perfection, and are ready to do what God demands, and to suffer all that He requires for holiness of life...................... 127
Affections.—Fear. Resolution...................... 128

SIXTH DAY.

Intermediate Meditation III.—On the third degree of humility, or the love of contempt.

POINT I.

It is just that we love contempt..................... 129
Affections.—An act of Self-abasement. Resolution.... 131

POINT II.

Our own interest requires that we love contempt...... 131
Affections.......... 133

POINT III.

Its very excellence requires that we love contempt..... 134
Affections.—Prayer to obtain the spirit of humility. ... 135

Meditation I.—On the interior sufferings of Christ in the Garden of Gethsemane.

POINT I.

Christ has led the way in suffering all the interior trials, which are met with on the road to perfection. 137
Affections.—Astonishment. Resolution............ 139

POINT II.

The state of dereliction is more profitable to us than that of consolation................................. 140
Affections.—Oblation. A prayer to obtain fortitude... 141

SEVENTH DAY.

Meditation II.—On the exterior sufferings of Jesus Christ while hanging on the cross.

POINT I.

We can never suffer in our bodies what Jesus has suffered in His body................................. 143
Affections.—Thanksgiving. Resolution............. 144

POINT II.

Christ's patience was as wonderful as His pains were terrible.. 145
Affections.—Self-confusion. Acknowledgment and Resolution.. 147

Meditation III.—On the affronts and outrages which Jesus suffered.

POINT I.

There never has been one and never will there be one who suffered such affronts and outrages as Jesus Christ.. 148
Affections.—Admiration of Jesus' meekness. Self-confusion.. 151

POINT II.

There never has been one and never will there be one who suffered outrages and insults in the manner in which Christ suffered them.......................... 152
Affections.—Esteem and Love of Contempt. Compunction and Resolution............................. 153

Meditation IV.—On the love which Christ on the cross has shown for His enemies.

POINT I.

The Love of Jesus was wonderful on account of the circumstances, and of the hatred and rage of His enemies... 154
Affections.—Self-abasement. Contrition.............. 157

POINT II.

The Love of Jesus was wonderful on account of the circumstances of His love........................ 158
Affections.—Compunction. Resolution and Supplication. 160
End of the third week. The soul is beginning to be prepared for union with God... 161

THE FOURTH WEEK.—THE UNITIVE WAY.

EIGHTH DAY

Meditation I.—On the Resurrection of Jesus Christ.

POINT I.

The happiness of His resurrection was as great as the bitterness of His suffering was terrible............ 166
Affections.—Rejoicing at the Glory of Jesus Christ. A desire of the same happiness...................... 168

POINT II.

Holy thoughts and resolutions that arise from the meditation on the Resurrection....................... 168
Affections.—An Act of Faith. Compunction. On the love of God...................................... 170

Meditation II.—God is infinitely good towards us.

POINT I.

God deserves to be loved on account of His being infinitely good to us here on earth.................. 171
Affections.—Admiration of the love of God. Compunction and An Act of Love....................... 173

POINT II.

God deserves to be loved on account of His being infinitely good to us hereafter........................ 174
Affections.—An Act of Love. Desire to love God perfectly... 175

Meditation III.—God is infinitely good in Himself.

POINT I.

God deserves to be loved, because He is the Supreme Good.. 176
Affections.—Confusion and Astonishment. Resolution and Compunction.................................. 179

POINT II.

God deserves to be loved, because He is the only Good. 180
Affections.—Confusion. An Act of Love and Oblation. Petition.. 182

SELF-EXAMINATION.

INTRODUCTORY REMARKS.

First Day.—Examination on Purity of Heart......... 188
Second Day.—Examination on Inordinate Love....... 194
Third Day.—Examination on the Desire of Esteem and Honor.................................... 199
Fourth Day.—Examination on Sloth and Sadness...... 203
Fifth Day.—Examination on Anger.................. 212
Sixth Day.—Examination on Inordinate Zeal......... 216
Seventh Day.—Examination on our Love for God..... 221
Eighth Day.—Examination on the Love of our Neighbor 229

FIRST DAY.

This day forms the groundwork of the retreat. Its meditations tend to two purposes:

1st. To make us thoroughly understand the end for which we were created; viz., to honor and love God in this world, and to enjoy Him forever in the next.

2d. To make us strenuously resolve to attain this end.

Meditation 1.

THE END OF MAN.

POINT I.

IT IS JUST TO LIVE CONFORMABLY TO YOUR END.

Go back, in imagination, a little, and remember that a hundred years ago you were nothing. God first created your body, and then breathed into it an immortal soul, and you were a human being. You are therefore the work of an Infinite Wisdom, of an Infinite Goodness, and thus wholly God's.

1st. You are a work of Infinite Wisdom. Infinite Wisdom cannot create anything without an end worthy of Itself. This end is no other than that you should know, honor, and love God in this world, and in the next see and enjoy Him forever. Your duty, therefore, has ever been, and ever will be, to honor and love God.

2d. You are a work of Infinite Goodness. Suppose yourself in the world, in the same state of life and with the same gifts you now enjoy, but that you are speechless. God loosens your tongue and enables you to speak, on this condition: Never henceforth to utter a word but for His honor and glory. Can there be anything more just than that this tongue should always praise Him who gave it the power of speech? Pause, and consider whether you have a sense of your body, or a faculty of your soul, which was not given you for a similar purpose.

3d. You are wholly God's. He has created you out of nothing, and He is consequently your Lord and Master. He who owns a garden, and has it tilled and planted, is the sole master of all that it produces. Whoever takes therefrom against his will is guilty of theft. It is a trite axiom, To the owner of the soil belong the fruits of it. God created you. He is therefore the Lord, and the Master of all that arises from you. To foster then a single affection which does not tend to His glory, to say or to do anything which is not in some way for His praise and love, is injustice. Servants are deserving of blame in the discharge of their duties in two ways. First, by remissness, or a superficial performance of their obligations. Secondly, by malice or the guilt of actual injury to those whom they serve. How have you served God, your Master? What does your conscience say?

AFFECTIONS.

Confession.—O my God, I see how sinful my life has been! My end was to honor and love Thee with my whole heart and soul; I should never have spent a moment, never spoken a word, never performed an action which tended not, in some way or other, to Thy honor. And what have I done! In what and for whom have the hours of my life been employed? On whom have the affections of my soul been centred? Ah! how much have I done for the creature, and how little for Thee, my Creator! Woe unto me! How tepid, how ungrateful, and how wicked have I been!

Contrition.—What now remains for me, O my God, but to implore Thy clemency and forgiveness? I detest my sins with my whole heart, and wish every day which has not been spent in Thy service to be blotted out from the number of my days.

POINT II.

IT IS ADVANTAGEOUS TO LIVE CONFORMABLY TO YOUR END.

The end for which God created you is not only for His own glory, to honor and love Him in this world, but also for your eternal happiness, to enjoy Him in the next. As truly as you are now living on earth, so truly will you one day dwell in heaven, if you serve God faithfully. Here pause and consider the happiness which awaits you.

1st. There is in heaven supreme happiness for the soul. To wish to understand the bliss which a soul enjoys in heaven would be as it were to drain the ocean of its waters. One thought, however, will help you to conceive in some way its extent. The happiness of God is infinite, and this infinite happiness is the end of your creation. God wishes you to partake of the same happiness which He Himself enjoys, and to share in the same glory which He Himself possesses.

2d. There is in heaven, likewise, a supreme happiness for the body. The soul does not alone serve God, but it is assisted frequently by the body. The body, therefore, must share the recompense awarded to the soul. But what tongue can express the happiness of the body? Happiness so great that, as the Apostle says, "Eye hath not seen, nor ear heard, neither hath it entered into the heart of man, what things God hath prepared for them that love Him."

3d. This happiness will last forever. How brief is earthly enjoyment, compared with heavenly? Long ere this there lived kings and queens, whose splendor dazzled millions, and whose sceptre made empires tremble. Where are they now? They are mouldering in the dust, and even trampled under foot. To-day there are potentates who are almost worshipped as deities; a hundred years hence what will remain of them? Nothing but a handful of dust, which the wind scatters at will. Not such is the glory that awaits you. Its duration is eternal. The joys which ravish all the faculties of the soul are eternal. That torrent of delights which inundates the senses of the body is eternal. All is without change, without cessation, forever.

AFFECTIONS.

Hope.—O Infinite Goodness! How consoling is this truth: Heaven is my country, my inheritance, eternally mine! If I honor and love God, a day will come in which I shall surpass the sun in brightness, in which I myself shall behold the heavenly paradise, where soul and body will be inebriated with the torrent of its delights. O blessed day! Dare I hope for thee? Yes, I hope for thee, and I hope for thee most confidently. God's promise is pledged thereunto.

Contempt of all temporal things.—If Heaven is mine, why do I not despise the world and all it offers? Why do I repine at the ills of the body, if this same body shall enjoy uninterrupted delights? Why does the contempt of men disquiet and afflict me, if I am to be esteemed and loved forever by God and His saints? O my God, I have been blind and have prized too highly the things of earth.

POINT III.

It is Necessary to Live Conformably to your End.

1st. God is Infinite Goodness and Infinite Justice. Engrave deeply the following truth on your mind: As His Goodness is Infinite, it is impossible for Him not to love and reward eternally those who honor Him, and as His Justice is Infinite, it is impossible for Him not to detest and punish eternally those who contemn Him.

2d. The Infinite Goodness of God created Heaven, and His Infinite Justice made Hell. In Heaven He will reward forever faithful souls, and they will praise and glorify Him forever; in hell He will hate and punish everlastingly unfaithful souls, and they will never cease to curse and blaspheme Him.

3d. Hence if you honor and love God on earth, your bliss in Heaven will eternally proclaim His mercy; if you refuse to honor and love Him on earth, your damnation shall exalt

His Justice in Hell. Heaven and earth will pass away, but His word shall not pass away. You will therefore either dwell forever in Heaven or suffer eternally in Hell. Your soul will either love or hate God unceasingly, for your soul is immortal. Your body will either enjoy the everlasting bliss of Heaven or suffer the eternal torments of Hell; for this body, being raised from the dead, will die no more.

AFFECTIONS.

Fear.—O my God! shall I be numbered among the blessed? O awful question which makes me shudder! Shall I be inebriated with the joys of Heaven? I know not; but this I know, that Thou, O Lord, hast said: "He that loveth his life shall lose it, and he that hateth his life in this world keepeth it unto life eternal" (St John xii. 25). These are Thy words. To love my life signifies to delight in sensual things, to follow the bent of my own will, to fly from contempt, to be displeased with those who offend me To hate my life means to mortify myself, to deny my own will, to accept willingly and even to seek contempt, to return good for evil. Have I acted thus until now? Woe is me! The words of my Saviour condemn me. I have not been of the number of those who hate their lives.

Resolution.—O my God, if to gain my end is to be eternally happy, and if to lose my end is to be eternally miserable, how can I be so careless in so important a matter? Should I not from this out gladly sacrifice the highest of earthly enjoyments, were it necessary, to purchase those of Heaven? Should I not from this out be willing to shed my blood, if necessary, in order to escape Hell? Most certainly to procure an infinite good, or to avoid an infinite evil, one can never do enough, and never suffer enough. O my God, prostrate in Thy presence, I resolve to gain my end, cost what it may. For this purpose I resolve to refuse no sacrifice. Whatever I shall discover in the course of these holy exercises to be useful or necessary to my soul, that I will do.

A Prayer to Employ Divine Grace.

How often have I taken these resolutions and how often have I broken them? I need, therefore, O God, Thy help; otherwise I shall be lost. I turn then to Thee, O Heavenly Father! Hearken to the cry of my heart. O Infinite Goodness, deal not with me according to my deserts, but according to Thy infinite mercy; deal not with me according to the severity of Thy Justice, but according to Thy Infinite Goodness and tender compassion.

Meditation 2.

THE END OF RELIGIOUS.

POINT I.

THE EXCELLENCE OF YOUR STATE REQUIRES OF YOU TO LIVE CONFORMABLY TO YOUR END.

Do you sufficiently comprehend its dignity? Your end is to honor and love God in this world; but in a higher degree, and in a more perfect manner, than seculars, and, in the next, to enjoy God eternally, but in a higher and more perfect degree of glory than seculars. Consider the advantages which this state possesses. The first advantage is the assurance of your salvation. If you live as your state requires, you would wrong God by entertaining the least doubt of your salvation. Listen to the promise He made: "Every one that hath left house, or brethren, or sisters, or father, or mother, or children, or lands, for my name's sake, shall receive a hundred-fold, and shall possess life everlasting" (St. Matthew xix. 29). Who is it that spoke thus? God, who in His words is Truth itself, and who is infinitely faithful to His promises. What can be more consoling than this?

The second advantage is sanctity, and union with God. On the day that God called you to a religious life He also called you to holiness.

He wished you to consecrate to Him, at that time, your soul, with all its faculties and affections. This was God's intention. For this purpose only He withdrew you from the turmoil of the world, and led you into the retirement of the cell, that He alone might reign as Sovereign Lord in your heart, inflame it with the ardor of His love, and prepare it, little by little, for the abode in which He with you and you with Him may live in the most tender familiarity.

The third advantage is a high degree of glory in Heaven. All the blessed in Heaven are sovereigns, and enjoy ineffable happiness. Still one exceeds another in glory, as the brilliancy of the sun surpasses the radiance of the smaller luminaries. To you, O Religious! belongs the glory which will exalt you above myriads of the elect; it is promised you; for you it is prepared. "If thou wilt be perfect," says the Eternal Truth, "go sell what thou hast, and give to the poor, and thou shalt have treasure in Heaven; and come, follow me" (St. Matt. xix. 21).

Picture to yourself an infant prince, heir to a kingdom. This child cannot appreciate his prerogative, but others gaze on him with veneration, esteem him happy, and regard his position as the most enviable one in the world. Nature has elevated him above millions of men, fortune has lavished on him its choicest gifts, so that his life will be spent in the enjoyment of the most refined pleasures. Were the eyes of your soul sufficiently enlightened, how much more enviable would your state of life appear? After a short lapse of time, you will have come to your inheritance; you will sit among the Angels, and a glorious crown will encircle your brow. You will be filled with delights, in comparison with which all the pleasures of the world will be naught but empty bubbles.

AFFECTIONS.

Esteem for Religious Vocation. — Is this, then, the end for which God led me into solitude? To know and love God in this life more fervently than seculars, and also to possess Him in the other life in a higher degree of glory? To be admitted to a more intimate friendship with Him, to love Him ardently, and to be loved by Him in return, and to commence here below the union which is to continue in Heaven without end? Oh! what a signal favor is this! Blessed and praised forever be such Infinite Goodness and mercy!

An Act of Self-abasement. — How much should this very favor humble me? It tells me to be meek and gentle; to bear in silence, and with tranquillity, the pains inflicted by my neighbor; to suffer contempt and humiliations without being troubled; to practise an obedience which makes me ready at every moment to submit my will to that of superiors; to be inflamed with so great a love of God as to spend hours in uninterrupted communion with Him. This is the perfection to which the grace of my vocation calls me. Do I correspond to it? What is my answer?

POINT II.

THE EXTRAORDINARY LOVE OF GOD FOR YOU REQUIRES OF YOU TO LIVE ACCORDING TO YOUR END.

To understand the greatness of His love, consider the following truths:

1st. God called you to the religious life with wonderful predilection. You did not choose Him, but He you. "You have not chosen Me," said Christ to His Apostles, "but I have chosen you." The first thought which you had of this sort of life, your first inclination towards it, the fortitude by which you conquered the obstacles, came purely from Him. The election was His, not yours; for, He without you would have been equally happy.

2d. God called you without your deserving this grace. How many millions have been left to battle with the dangers and temptations of the world, who would have served God better than you? Nevertheless God has left them and chosen you.

3d. God called you to a religious life, though others, if chosen, would have paid Him greater honor and glory. How many millions live in the world who will be irretrievably lost; all of them would have been saved, had God conferred on them the graces He has lavished on you! How many thousands are there in the world who would have attained an eminent degree of sanctity, had they received the same grace of vocation as you? But His foreknowledge did not incline Him to prefer them to you. On you He cast His eyes and drew you to Himself.

ＡＦＦＥＣＴＩＯＮＳ.

Gratitude.—How boundless is Thy goodness and mercy to me, O my God! How much hast Thou done to lead me to You? Tens of thousands would have more faithfully corresponded to Your graces, and through them would have reached perfection. Thou hast overlooked them, and chosen me. O incomprehensible Love! How much do I owe Thee?

An Act of Self-abasement.—The nobler and the more exalted religious life is, the greater is my ingratitude. How many persons live in the world who, for all their life, obey the commands of pitiless masters without murmuring, while I cannot do the will of God, the best of masters, even in the most trifling matters? How many who for whole years are pinched by poverty, who are calumniated, despised, and sorely persecuted, and who nevertheless bear all in silence, and submit cheerfully to the will of God, while I complain, and shrink from the least cross. O Jesus! How much art Thou offended by me! since fewer graces have brought forth so much fruit in these souls, and in me Thy multiplied graces have produced little or none! Shall not the words of Thy threat be verified in me: "Behold, they are last that shall be first, and they are first that shall be last" (St. Luke xiii. 30).

POINT III.

IT IS ABSOLUTELY NECESSARY FOR YOU TO LIVE ACCORDING TO YOUR END.

You must honor and love God, but in a higher degree and in a more perfect manner than persons living in the world. This is the obligation which God imposes on you. How will it fare with you, if you fail to comply with it? Alas! miserably, my soul, miserably, whether God deals with you according to His Mercy, or according to His Justice.

1st. If God deals with you according to His Mercy, you may attain unto salvation, but in an inferior degree, and after undergoing protracted sufferings in Purgatory. I say, in an inferior degree. God hath prepared for you an exalted throne in Heaven, but since you render yourself unworthy of it by your tepidity, He will deprive you of the clear light of your understanding, of the tender inclinations of your heart; He will deprive you of the extraordinary graces wherewith He would have enriched you, and will bestow them on an humble servant, on a pious widow, or on a poor beggar, who will employ them in fervently serving Him. I say, moreover, only after protracted sufferings in Purgatory. It is certain that the tepid Religious commits innumerable venial sins. It is certain that each day increases their number. It is certain that every venial sin, if not atoned for in this life, must be expiated in the fire of Purgatory. How long this suffering may last, no one can say, and judge thence what your condition will be after a long life of tepidity, even if God deals with you according to His Mercy.

2d. But if God treats you according to His Justice, then you may look upon your perdition as inevitable, but it will be far more terrible, than that of persons dying in the world.

I say first, your perdition is inevitable. "The earth," says the Holy Ghost, "that drinketh in the rain which cometh often upon it, and which bringeth forth thorns and briars, is reprobate, and very near unto a curse" (Heb. vi. 7).

This earth is your soul, which has been inundated with showers of heavenly graces and inspirations such as to lead readily to sanctity. What will then happen? The land will be left barren and accursed.

I say secondly, perdition more terrible than that of persons living in the world awaits you. The more ardent God's love is for a soul in this world, the more severe is His Justice in the next, if His love is contemned. The more generous is His liberality here on earth, the greater is His anger hereafter, if His graces are abused. Witness the withering threats pronounced against those unfortunate cities, which had received so many graces from Christ, and with which they did not correspond: "Wo to thee, Corazain; wo to thee, Bethsaida; for if in Tyre and Sidon had been wrought the miracles that have been wrought in you, they had long ago done penance in hair-cloth and ashes. But I say unto you, it shall be more tolerable for Tyre and Sidon in the day of judgment than for you. And thou, Capharnaum, shalt thou be exalted up to Heaven? Thou shalt go down even unto Hell" (St. Matt. xi. 21). When Christ acts according to His Justice, the unfortunate Religious, who would have been higher in Heaven, sink lower in Hell.

AFFECTIONS.

Fear.—O my God! shall I be saved? Shall I ever see Thee? A tepid, unmortified life cannot save me. So long as love is not ardent, prayer fervent, mortification earnest, my salvation is not sure. Countless numbers have been lost who were less tepid than I, but on account of their abuse of grace, God withheld from them His final assistance. O Jesus! My lukewarmness has deserved nothing else but that I be rejected by Thee.

Resolution.—But how long, O my God! shall I delay? Alas! Too many years have I spent in tepidity, and too many graces I have abused. It is time that I arise from my torpor, and earnestly set about the work of my perfection. Now, O Jesus! this very hour I will begin to serve Thee as Thou desirest.

Love.—Is it possible for me ever to love God perfectly? Yes, it is possible. O consoling assurance! Now, this very hour, I can love Thee,

O God! perfectly. I turn therefore my whole heart to Thee, O Infinite Being. Would that I could combine in my heart the ardent love of the heavenly spirits! From this out I will retrieve lost time, and hasten to life everlasting. I resolve to do everything during these days, that I know to be agreeable unto Thee. Foster this my love of Thee, O Jesus, and stir it up, by Thy grace, to a lively flame.

Meditation 3.

On Complete Indifference towards Creatures.

Eternal salvation may be lost, either through an inordinate attachment to some created things or through aversion for others. The first are earthly comforts, or the gratification of the senses, wealth, honor and esteem of men. The others are poverty, suffering, contempt, sickness, and premature death. If, then, you desire to secure your last end, you must renounce all natural inclinations and aversions for things of this sort, being ready to sacrifice whatever is most pleasant, should it be an obstacle to your salvation, and to enter upon any undertaking, however painful to nature, which will help you to obtain your soul's eternal welfare.

POINT I.

GOD'S SUPREME DOMINION REQUIRES OF YOU TO KEEP YOURSELF IN A STATE OF PERFECT INDIFFERENCE.

The end of your existence in this world is, to honor and love God perfectly; but to honor and love God perfectly means nothing but to fulfil exactly His holy will. Now this cannot be done, unless the heart be equally disposed to accept health or sickness, esteem or contempt.

Reflect then seriously on the following truths:

1st. God, not you, must determine the manner in which you have to serve Him. You must serve Him as He wills, not as you please. He is the Master, and you the servant. The master's right is to command, the servant's duty is to obey. Even in the heavenly hierarchies this order is observed. Some of the Angels sing unceasingly before the throne of God canticles of praise, others attend and protect men; some are guardians of the just, others of the wicked: each serves God as he is commanded. Should God exercise less dominion on earth than in heaven?

2d. The supreme dominion of God is to prescribe to you the manner of serving Him. He is God and you are His creature. Who can or dare circumscribe His power? The potter does with his work what he lists; he puts it where he wishes, uses it for the meanest purposes; he breaks it into pieces; in short, disposes of it as he fancies. Should God be denied the same right to treat man whom He created, that the potter has over the work of his hands?

3d. You serve God as He wills, when you honor and love Him perfectly, in the condition in which He has placed you.

If you are intrusted with an office, you must discharge its duties earnestly, assiduously, and cheerfully, for the pure love of God. This is what *loving and serving God as He wills* means. If your soul is full of darkness, and a prey to temptations, sadness, and spiritual dereliction, you must bend beneath the cross, and kiss, as it were, the hand that strikes you. If you are hated, despised, and calumniated, you must drink the bitter chalice without complaint, for such is the will of your Heavenly Father. The farther you stray from this path, the more difficult your road to Heaven will become.

AFFECTIONS.

Acknowledgment of the Dominion of God. —O Supreme Good! to Thee belongs the right to command. I am Thy creature, whose duty is to obey. I must honor and love Thee, but not as I will, but as Thou wilt. I acknowledge Thy supreme dominion, and humbly bow down before it. Woe to those who presume to serve God according to their caprice. To serve God as they will, not as He wills, is to make themselves the masters, and to degrade the great God to the condition of a servant.

Sorrow and Contrition.—How is it possible that poor mortals can be found to act so contrary to reason? Alas! even the religious state has too many such. I myself have been one of them; this I confess to my shame. I desire to love and serve Thee in good health; in sickness I like not to serve Thee. I will honor and love Thee as long as I possess the affection and esteem of men, but in neglect and disgrace I am unwilling to serve Thee. I am anxious to love and worship Thee as long as I enjoy interior peace, and while sensible devotion dilates my heart, but in aridity and temptation I care not for serving Thee and forget Thee.

POINT II.

THE PROVIDENCE OF GOD REQUIRES OF YOU TO KEEP YOURSELF IN COMPLETE INDIFFERENCE.

As it is difficult to reach our final end without this holy indifference, so it is easy with it. To understand this better, consider the following truths:

1st. God is Infinite Wisdom, and knows what means will conduct you surely to your last end. Everything may contribute to it, viz.: health or sickness, honor or contempt, an honorable or abject office—all may be used as means, when used properly. Tell me now, which is the better means to lead you more safely to your last end, to be strong and healthy in body, or to be disabled by infirmities, to be loaded with honors or to be the object of unmerited contempt and calumny, to be engaged in an honorable or low employment? This is a secret which bids defiance to the human intellect, an abyss whose depths no mortal eye can fathom, a mystery which is unveiled only for God Omnipotent.

2d. God is Infinite Love. As long as the soul remains in this indifference, He always ordains for it the most efficacious means to reach its last end. God is to the soul what a mother is to the child. Sooner would the most affectionate mother force her offspring to swallow a deadly potion than would God ordain anything hurtful to the soul that abandons itself entirely to Him. This is an incontestable truth. If God visits you with sickness, if He permits you to be despised and persecuted, if He leaves your soul in darkness, temptation, and dereliction, these are the means which shall prove most effective in enabling you to gain your last end.

3d. God is Infinite Power, and infallibly conducts the soul to its last end, as long as it perseveres in this indifference. Who can understand the power of the Omnipotent? Neither angel nor man, neither heaven, earth, nor hell, can prevail against His power. You alone are capable of putting obstacles in the way, if you withdraw yourself from the direction of God's providence. But, on the contrary, if you persevere in allowing yourself to be guided by it, God will conduct you surely to your end, Infinite Wisdom, Infinite Love, and Infinite Power as He is.

AFFECTIONS.

Confidence.—How consoling is this thought: He who governs me is Wisdom itself, and He knows what means are the most sure. He who loves me is the fountain of all love, and at every moment ordains that which is best for me. He who guides me is Infinite Power, and when His hand supports and defends, no power can enfeeble or injure. Should I then not banish all diffidence from my heart? With perfect confidence I throw myself into the arms of Thy fatherly care, O God! I cry out to Thee: Thou wishest me to share with Thee the bliss of Heaven, where Thou hast prepared for me an exalted throne of glory. As great as this Thy favor is, so is the ardor of my hope. Thou art my Father, and Thy love shall conduct me to eternal happiness.

Self-abasement.—How can I hope for this happiness? It is only for those who honor and love Thee as Thou willest, and who keep themselves in a spirit of perfect indifference. Am I one of these? Alas! how elated am I when warmed by the sun of sensible consolations? How troubled when its rays are obscured by the clouds of dereliction and temptations! How joyfully do I obey one command, and how reluctantly another!

POINT III.

THE JUSTICE OF GOD REQUIRES OF YOU TO KEEP YOURSELF IN COMPLETE INDIFFERENCE.

If you do not with humble submission employ the means which God prescribes for your last end, His Justice will overtake you. Hence will follow incalculable misfortunes.

1st. You will have to suffer incomparably more than if you were fortified by a spirit of indifference. You are sadly in error if you imagine you can evade the troubles and afflictions which the love of God has ordained as means to your end. These pains and temptations, that contempt and persecution, which He has appointed for you, you must endure. Now, let us suppose you are indifferent and bear these trials patiently. You then have this testimony, that you please God (Heb. xi. 5), who both strengthens you with an increase of grace by making your cross light and sweet; but if you have not this indifference, and unwillingly bear the cross, you displease God. He withdraws His helping hand from you and allows you to pine away unaided beneath its heavy weight.

2d. You forfeit everlastingly the exalted degree of glory which would have been yours by God's eternal decree. It is impossible to attain to your end, except by the path which God has traced out. Were you to refuse to tread cheerfully this path, you would toil in vain, you would never reach the goal.

3d. Your very salvation is in danger. A soul that has not this indifference is necessarily subject to many and grievous temptations. At one time it gives way either to anger and melancholy or to sadness and diffidence; at another time it is swayed by pride and the fear of contempt. All the unsubdued passions spring up, sometimes simultaneously, at other times separately. To put down such foes as these requires the help of the God of armies. Will He succor in its afflictions a soul that withdraws itself from His guidance, that spurns the weapons He furnishes, that will acknowledge no law in His service but its own caprice?

AFFECTIONS.

Act of Humility.—My Lord and my God! in what a piteous state my soul is! What darkness in my understanding, what disorder in my will! I look upon pains and sickness as the greatest evils, and Thou regardest them as the surest means of my sanctification. I consider temptations as the most deplorable misfortunes, and Thou seest in them so many steps to my exaltation in Heaven. I imagine that dereliction is my ruin, and Thou remindest me that if it be borne with resignation, it will be the brightest gem in my crown of glory. My judgment then leads me astray! Alas! this is not all: as my understanding is blind, so is my will perverse. The love of honor and esteem, the desire of comfort and of rest, these captivate my heart. Eagerly do I grasp the poisoned cup and fling from me the sole antidote which could restore my health.

Resolution.—I have clearly perceived these two things: 1st. I must honor and love Thee as Thou wilt, not as I will. 2d. I cannot honor and love Thee thus unless I be indifferent and employ the means which Thou hast appointed; neither can I secure my salvation and attain unto sanctity. I, therefore, divest myself of every attachment to creatures, and of every repugnance for them; honor or contempt, health or sickness, consolation or dryness, this or that command of my superiors, all shall henceforth be alike to me. Let nature repine and murmur; from this time forward Thy grace will prevail. This is my resolution, O my God!

A PRAYER TO IMPLORE GRACE.

How happy I am to have at last laid the corner-stone! My soul is now stamped with the characteristic of sanctity. I tread the path which will conduct to union with God. But who shall keep me in this state? Surely not myself; my weakness is too great and my inconstancy too manifest. Thy Omnipotence alone can sustain my infirmity. To Thee, therefore, I raise my whole soul, and I cry out: "O Jesus! root out from my heart every attachment to creatures which flatters my self-sufficiency, and remove every repugnance which wounds self-love. Grant me to desire nothing but to please Thee, and to fear nothing but to offend Thee."

FIRST WEEK.

THE PURGATIVE WAY.

To-day opens the first week of the spiritual exercises. It contains five meditations. Its end is: 1st. To consider in the light of faith the heinousness of sin. 2d. To bring to mind the multitude and grievousness of the sins of your life, and to bewail them sincerely. 3d. To take a firm resolution to die rather than to commit a mortal sin, which is the only evil that leads you away from your last end.

SECOND DAY.

Meditation 1.

ON THE SIN OF THE REBEL ANGELS AND THAT OF OUR FIRST PARENTS.

POINT I.

THE PUNISHMENT OF THE REBEL ANGELS SHOWS WHAT AN INFINITE EVIL SIN IS.

Go back in imagination to the time when God created Heaven and filled it with angels. Who could be happier than these blessed spirits? Their beauty was so ravishing that no mortal eye could have beheld it without dying of joy; their wisdom so exalted that Solomon's is but ignorance compared with theirs. They were incapable of suffering, their happiness was without alloy; their abode as pleasant as the heavenly Paradise. The gifts of their nature were great, but the gifts of grace were still greater. God had infused into their souls a perfect knowledge and an ardent love of Himself. Some of the angels abused the gifts of God's goodness. They did not serve Him as He willed, they sinned, and were immediately punished.

The circumstances of this punishment were:

1st. It was a privation of all good. The rebellious angels were changed from the most beautiful spirits into the most hideous demons. Formerly they were the beloved children of God, now they became the object of His eternal wrath and hatred.

2d. It was an accumulation of all evils. They were hurled down like lightning from the highest heaven and plunged into the abyss of hell. There they suffer inconceivable torments. Their memory is racked by the most galling recollections; their understanding is clouded by their pride; their will the sport of ceaseless despair.

3d. It was sudden and immediate. Had God granted to those unhappy spirits but a moment, they might have acknowledged and abhorred their sin, and loved Him ardently for all eternity, but Divine Justice willed it not. No sooner was the crime committed than the chastisement followed without a moment for reflection.

4th. It was without satisfaction. These accursed spirits had suffered many thousands of years the torments of Hell, when Christ came into the world to destroy sin. Did he put an end to their torments or bring them any alleviation? Our merciful Lord, who shed so many tears over the city of Jerusalem, dropped not one to mitigate their tortures. The crime was momentary, the chastisement eternal.

Here pause and comtemplate in spirit the excruciating sufferings of these reprobate angels. Their aspect is so loathsome and so frightful, that no mortal could behold them without dying through terror. Then say to yourself: These demons were formerly spirits of transcendent beauty and masterpieces of Divine Omnipotence. What horrid crime have they committed to bring upon themselves this misfortune? They yielded to a thought of pride; they sinned once, and for this one sin alone they have already suffered thousands of years, and their torments shall never cease. Who has passed such a frightful sentence on them? God, . . . O dreadful truth! Then either God is not Infinite Wisdom, Infinite Justice, and Infinite Mercy, or sin is an infinite evil which cannot be sufficiently deplored.

AFFECTIONS.

Admiration.—O my God, my only and Supreme Good, what shall I now most admire—the severity of Thy Justice in chastising the rebel angels, or the excess of Thy Mercy towards me?

These heavenly spirits committed only one sin, and for this one sin Thou hast forever cast them from Thee, and I, but a handful of dust, have committed hundreds, perhaps thousands of sins, and Thou hast spared me. I have abused Thy Mercy, and after Thou hast pardoned me my sins, again and again have I raised my hand against Thee and said: I will not serve Thee; and still Thou hast pardoned me again. Even now Thou regardest me with eyes of affection and stretchest out to me the hands of Thy Mercy.

Contrition.—This unbounded mercy fills my heart with sorrow. I have offended God, who has loved me more than He has those myriads of angels. I have offended God who, in the midst of my iniquities, has shielded me with the buckler of His Mercy. I have offended God who, notwithstanding the multitude of my sins, will never cease to love me throughout eternity. O ungrateful heart, how couldst thou despise such love and offend such goodness ! Bitter sobs and tears should be my food day and night.

POINT II.

THE PUNISHMENT OF OUR FIRST PARENTS ALSO SHOWS THE INFINITE EVIL OF SIN.

The world has never witnessed greater happiness than that of our first parents.

1st. Their abode was a beautiful and most delightful paradise. In it there was neither heat nor cold to mar their joys, neither rain nor wind interrupted the pleasant sunshine; the trees produced, spontaneously, the richest fruits, the earth every variety of plants and flowers.

2d. They had full dominion over the brute creation. The birds obeyed their call, the beasts approached at their beck and crouched at their feet; a single word brought the fishes to the surface of the waters.

3d. The happiness of their bodies was complete. All around them throve without their care; they were strangers to labor and fatigue, to pains and infirmities, to old age and death. They had but to eat of the tree of life to maintain their bodies in the bloom of health.

4th. The happiness of their souls was inconceivable. The passions were wholly subject to reason; neither anger, sadness, envy, hatred, nor any inordinate passion disturbed the peace of their minds; they were blessed with a profound knowledge and ardent love of God; lastly, they were cheered by the promise that after a happy career, without sickness or death, they would exchange the garden of Eden for the court of Heaven, and reign with God eternally. Despite the liberality of God they proved ungrateful, their crime was the more heinous, as the generosity of their benefactor was boundless. They sinned, and condign punishment overtook them.

Consider now the circumstances of this punishment.

1st. For this one sin they lost the happiness of

Eden. The earth was cursed, and became barren unless it would be moistened by the sweat of their brows; it brought forth nothing but briars and brambles; they were cursed in their bodies and condemned to suffering, sickness, and a bitter death, and likewise cursed in their souls, they became enemies to God, and were banished from Paradise to this vale of tears.

2d. For this one sin all future generations were condemned to similar misery. Paradise is forfeited and we live on this earth full of sorrows; life is full of bitterness and death full of fear and terror; salvation is doubtful, and we cannot regain heaven but by tears and penance.

3d. For this one sin the greater number of persons in the world will be damned for all eternity. All who shall be condemned will incur damnation on account of the uncontrolled passions of their souls which drag them into sin; and the violence of their evil propensities is but the continuance of the punishment for the sin of our first parents.

4th. For this one sin Jesus had to die on the cross. O stupendous wonder! The Supreme Lord of heaven and earth was condemned to death—to the ignominious death of the cross.

AFFECTIONS.

Fear.—Faith reveals to me terrific truths. The most beautiful angels were cast out of heaven, the whole human race excluded from Paradise, and so many thousand millions of souls condemned to the flames of hell! Jesus, the Son of God, died on the Cross at the command of His Father, and all this for one only sin. O Sin, what an infinite evil is hidden in thee! But since the Heavenly Father treated His only begotten Son so severely, how will He treat us who have committed so many and so grievous sins? How will He treat us who have remained in a state of sin for such a length of time, and who have so often relapsed after having been so often pardoned?

Contrition.—O my God, no hope for me remains but in Thy infinite mercy, no remedy but in my repentance. I prostrate myself before Thee and detest with my whole soul all my sins. I never should have offended so good a God; I should rather have sacrificed a thousand lives, if I had them, than be guilty of such foul ingratitude. Oh! give my heart intense sorrow, and to my eyes a fountain of tears.

POINT III.

REFLECTIONS WHICH NECESSARILY FOLLOW THE CONSIDERATION OF THESE TRUTHS.

Collect all the powers of your soul and engrave on your mind the following points:

1st. If only one sin is such an abomination in the sight of God, what an abomination in His eyes must the sins of my soul be? If I have committed only one sin, I am necessarily loathed by

Almighty God in such a manner as he loathes one rebel angel. If I have committed a hundred sins, He must necessarily hate me alone, as much as He hates a hundred rebel angels.

2d. If but one sin deserves the punishment of hell, should I not praise the mercy of God? If I have committed but one sin, I have deserved hell as much as the rebel angels; if I have committed more than one sin, then I deserved hell more than these reprobate spirits; and why do I not now share their torments? That God who has visited them in His justice has extended to me His mercy! O wonderful forbearance!

3d. If God has punished so rigorously but one sin of the Angels and of men, should I not fear His justice? God has condemned to hell for all eternity so many millions of spirits for one sin, for one thought, for the fault of a moment, without granting them one instant for repentance. Were I to sin once more, could He not punish me with the same inexorable severity?

AFFECTIONS.

Compunction.—Heaven and earth are witnesses of the infinite hatred which Thou, O my God! bearest against sin. Would that only one drop of this hatred were to flow into my heart! No being deserves to be loved as much as Jesus; nothing deserves to be hated so much as sin; but I in my folly have hated Jesus and loved sin. O my God! I acknowledge and bewail my wickedness. Would that I had become the food of worms ere I had sinned! I have sinned; I have often and greatly sinned. O Jesus! grant me Thy pardon.

Thanksgiving.—My extreme malice recalls to my mind Thy immense mercy. Alas! I remember but too well the hour in which I committed my first sin! Hadst Thou, O my God, then treated me like the angels, I would now be suffering in hell! I shudder at the bare recollection of this thought. Thy mercies, O Lord, are exceeding great! Oh what thanks do I not owe Thee!

Supplication.—Have mercy on me, O Lord, according to Thy great mercy! I now plainly see what an infinite evil sin is. I find it in the punishment of the damned spirits; I discern it in the misery and the misfortunes of mankind; I behold it in the torments and agony of Jesus, who dies on a cross. By that blood which Thou, O Jesus! hast shed for my sins, grant me the grace to weep bitterly over my past sins, and henceforth to fly from sin as from death itself.

Meditation 2.

ON ACTUAL OR PERSONAL SINS.

POINT I.

WE MAY JUDGE OF THE INFINITE MALICE OF SIN FROM ITS EFFECTS.

What are its effects? Consider them well and be astonished:

1st. The instant that sin is committed the soul is changed from the most beautiful image of God into a most loathsome phantom. It is impossible to comprehend the loveliness of the soul when it is adorned with sanctifying grace: it is the reflection of the Divine Beauty itself. A saint to whom God once manifested the beauty of a soul, unsullied by sin, exclaimed: "I would give a thousand lives to save one such soul." But let the beauty of it be ever so enrapturing, it becomes equally deformed and hideous through sin. A sinful soul and a reprobate spirit are two phantoms which rival each other in deformity, and as no man could see the devil as he is, so also no man could behold a soul deformed by sin without dying of fright.

2d. The instant sin is committed, the soul becomes for God the object of the greatest hatred. No intellect in heaven or on earth can fathom the hatred with which God detests sin, and what an infinite loathing He has for it. God hates sin, and must hate it; for as God is, necessarily, infinitely good, so He must necessarily, with an infinite hatred, hate sin, which is an infinite evil.

3d. The instant sin is committed, the soul from a child of God becomes the slave of the devil. It is a sad misfortune to be possessed by the devil, and to carry in one's body day and night this eternally cursed denizen of hell; what must it then be, when the soul hands itself over by its perverse will to the devil to be his slave? One whose body is possessed by him may still remain a child of God, and can hope to enjoy Him eternally in heaven; but one whose soul is possessed by the devil is an enemy of God, and is every moment in danger of being dragged by his master to the eternal prison.

4th. The moment the soul has been stained by sin it sinks into the most abject degradation. There is nothing more pernicious than sin and nothing more contemptible than a sinful soul. Only imagine if God should open the eyes of all who meet you, so that they might see your soul, with all the sins and crimes which you have committed during your whole life in thought, word, and deed! O God! what shame, what confusion would be yours! Would you not rather hide yourself perpetually in darkness than encounter the gaze of any one? Oh! how much then should you be overwhelmed with confusion in God's presence! For under His very eye you have committed your sins, and the same eye always beholds the accumulated filth of your life according to that of Holy Writ: "All their iniquities are in the sight of God" (Eccl. xvii. 17).

AFFECTIONS.

Confusion.—How numerous are my sins, O my God! There is not a power of my soul, not a sense of my body, which I have not employed in offending and outraging Thee! Wretched memory! how many evil remembrances hast thou cherished! O cursed understanding! how many bad thoughts hast thou entertained! O depraved will! how many disorderly affections hast thou fostered! O sinful tongue! how many uncharitable and profane words hast thou uttered! If then, O my God! one sin alone causes Thy indignation and wrath, how must my soul appear in thy sight, covered, as it is, with so many crimes? Whither shall I go to hide my shame? O sin! how enticing thou art when thou bringest us to thy embrace! but oh how revolting, how loathsome, when we see thee as thou art! In truth, were I known as God knows me, there is not one on earth who would not turn in horror from me.

A Prayer to Implore Grace.—Ashamed of my folly, I stand before Thee, O my God! in dread and confusion. But to whom, O my God! shall I turn save to Thee, who art Goodness itself and infinite Mercy? Pierce my heart with bitter compunction, and cleanse thereby the filth of my soul; without the help of a special grace

I cannot feel this hearty sorrow; do not refuse me it, O Lord! that heaven and earth may have a further reason to praise Thy mercy.

POINT II.

WE ALSO LEARN THE INFINITE MALICE OF SIN FROM THE ABJECT STATE OF ONE WHO OFFENDS GOD.

Consider well what you are.

1st. There is no good in yourself. What are you in very truth? A handful of clay. Some years ago you were a mere nothing, and in a very short time you will be eaten up by worms, and will again return to dust. You are a creature, so contemptible that no created intellect can comprehend your vileness; neither the Blessed Virgin's nor the holy angels' can penetrate the abyss of your nothingness. God alone fathoms it. And yet, handful of dust and worm of the earth as you are, you have raised your hands against God; you dared despise Him and say: "Who is the Lord, that I should hear His voice?" (Exod. v. 2.) I know no master and acknowledge none.

2d. You are one to whom God has been infinitely liberal. God has conferred on you innumerable benefits; not a single instant of your life has passed without His bestowing on you another blessing; every moment of eternity, if you will it so, God will lavish on you still further favors. He has done and will do all this with an eternal love, for He has not loved Himself more than you.

He has cherished you with a gratuitous love, for He does not stand in need of you or of your works; with a generous love, for He could have showered these graces upon others who would have served Him more faithfully. And yet you were so bold as often to offend Him, your God and your greatest benefactor! What a shameful act it would be for a son to so far forget himself as to outrage his father by maltreating him? Are you not equally ungrateful, O contemptible being, to the best of fathers—to your Heavenly Father?

Whatever there is in you, you owe it to your Creator; He gave it to you and He must preserve it for you. What shocking ingratitude on your part, is it not, to abuse the very gifts of God, and to turn them against Himself? What would you think of the dumb man, had he blasphemed our Lord on the cross with the very tongue which was miraculously loosened by His Omnipotence? Think thus of yourself. For who has given you all the senses of your body, and all the faculties of your soul, and yet have you not used them all to offend the Being who gave you them?

3d. You are one whom God has rescued from the frightful dungeon of hell. Had you committed but one sin, you would have deserved hell, and you owe to the mercy of God that you have not been plunged into its flames. Thus faith teaches. How immensely this increases your guilt! Were God to free a reprobate from hell and to grant him time for penance, and yet, notwithstanding this infinite benefit, this spirit would blaspheme again, do you not believe that he would deserve hell more than once? God has saved you from damnation ten, twenty, thirty times—ay, oftener; and after so much mercy what have you done in return?

AFFECTIONS.

Self-abasement.—O Dearest Lord! I cast myself in spirit into the abyss of Hell; for what other place could I find that suits me better? I, a lump of clay, dared rise in rebellion against the Sovereign Being from whom I have received all that I am and all that I have. And still He spares me. O wretched and condemned Angels! you are not more unfortunate than I, because you have sinned more; but you are unhappier than I, because God was less merciful to you than to me. So much time has been given to me, while none has been granted to you. You have committed but one sin, and I a number of sins; you had only one grace, and I so many thousands; God rejected you after one sin, and He wished to pardon me after so many offences. Should not a fountain of tears flow from my eyes, to bewail my sins all the days of my life?

Compunction.—O Sovereign Lord, who triest the hearts and the reins, I hate and abhor, with all my soul, the sins that I have committed up to this moment. Would that all the sorrow and compunction which holy penitents ever felt, were in my heart that I might the better deplore them! Instead of my sorrow I offer to Thee the bitterness and the anguish which Jesus felt, and the bloody sweat which He endured for my transgressions.

POINT III.

THE SUPREME MAJESTY OF GOD WHO IS OFFENDED PLAINLY SHOWS WHAT AN INFINITE EVIL SIN IS.

The greater the dignity of the person who is offended, the more grievous is the offence. Weigh now the enormity of sin. What is God?

1st. God is an infinite Good. He is a Being who contains in Himself all perfections. He is infinite Goodness, infinite Power, infinite Sanctity, infinite Beauty, infinite Mercy and infinite Liberality. He is the Supreme Good in Himself, and the source of all good in created things; there is no power, no goodness, no sanctity, no beauty, no mercy, no liberality, neither in Heaven nor on Earth, which does not flow from God as from its only fountain. Knowingly and willingly to offend, despise, and outrage such a Supreme Good, what malice must not this be?

2d. God is an infinite majesty. Lift up your eyes to Heaven. God is seated on His throne, many thousand millions of Angels and Saints surround it; enshrined in the splendor of His majesty, they praise and magnify Him with all their strength, and as they see that they cannot praise Him as much as His Greatness deserves, they cast down their crowns and confess that He is worthy of infinitely more honor and love than they can give. At the same time a vile worm of the earth rises up, attacks, insults, and outrages His Supreme Majesty. How frightful is its malice! Oh, my soul! This is inconceivable and unutterable. Two ideas will give us a better understanding of it. 1st. Imagine that all the Angels descend from Heaven and assume human bodies; that all men who ever lived from the beginning of the world up to this time, rise from their graves, and that all these live a thousand years and perform the most rigorous penance, and at last, through love for God, in the most excruciating torments, shed every drop of their blood, could they by this repair the injury which one single sin inflicts on our God? No. It is impossible. 2nd. Were the Angels throughout eternity to use their intelligence in order to fathom the malice of sin, they could never fully comprehend this malice.

AFFECTIONS.

Self-accusation.—Enlightened by grace, O my God! I plainly see the depth of my malice. I have offended Thee. I, who am not an Angel, but a miserable creature, a clod of clay, a worm of the earth, I have offended Thee. And who art Thou? The Supreme Good, the source of every Good, the Sovereign Lord of Heaven and Earth. I have offended Thee! Where? Not in secret, not in Thy absence, but in the light of day, in Thy presence, in the midst of the splendor of Thy omniscient majesty. I have offended Thee! with what? with all the faculties of the soul and all the senses of the body, and even the very heart which Thou hast given me solely to love Thee. And why have I offended Thee? Not in hope of a kingdom, not through fear of a cruel death, but for a paltry gratification of my senses, or through dread of a little confusion. I have offended Thee! How often? Not once alone, but more than once—often. Alas! too often I have offended Thee! When? At the very time in which Thou hast preserved my body in good health, in which Thou hast inundated my soul with new lights of grace, lest my enemy and Thine might drag me on to my eternal ruin. How great is my effrontery, my ingratitude and folly.

Compunction.—I have lived and offended Thee thus, and how have I repented? I have now and then made an act of contrition, struck my breast, and after this I have lived in security as if I were assured of Thy forgiveness. Should I be satisfied with this trifling and short-lived contrition? Should not my heart be continually filled with sorrow and my eyes with tears? I have offended an infinite Good. This is enough for unceasing sorrow! O God, worthy of all love, would that I never had offended Thee. I am fully resolved never more to offend Thee. Behold me now contrite at Thy feet! I beseech Thee, by the blood of Jesus Christ, to have pity on me. I resolve, in Thy presence, rather to die than to sin again. Yes, O Jesus! Thou art the Lord of life and death; if Thou forseest that I shall offend Thee mortally, take me out of this world before this misfortune befall me, Thy ungrateful servant.

Meditation 3.

ON THE FIRST PAIN OF HELL.—THE PAIN OF LOSS.

POINT I.

THE DAMNED IN HELL LOSE GOD, THEIR SOVEREIGN GOOD AND THEIR SUPREME HAPPINESS.

As it is impossible to comprehend what an infinite good it is to possess God, so it is impossible to understand what an infinite evil it is to lose Him. Let us try, however, as far as in us lies, to form some idea thereof. Enter, therefore, into yourself, and consider what it is to lose God.

1st. The damned are deprived of the Beatific Vision. As soon as the soul leaves the body, God infuses into it such a light as to comprehend the abyss of His Being, as far as a creature can; it conceives such a desire to possess God, that an instant of delay causes it excessive pain, and be-

On the First Pain of Hell.   65

cause it desires this possession most ardently, and cannot have this enjoyment, since it left the body in a state of mortal sin, there arises in it such bitterness and grief, that all the other torments of Hell are not to be compared to this loss.

2d. The providence of God takes no further care of the damned. As long as they lived on Earth, God provided for their wants; He put good thoughts into their minds, and enkindled holy desires in their hearts. But when He casts them off, all this care ceases. For this reason they shall, through eternity, never have a good thought, never feel a single good impulse, never have a single good desire, and never do a single good work. There will be in their imagination only horrible representations, in their understanding only fearful thoughts, in their memory only saddening pictures of the past, and in their will only raging madness.

3d. Since God cares for the damned no longer, no created being has any regard for them. The Blessed Virgin, the Guardian Angels and all the Saints loved them as long as they were here below, but when they are rejected by God, then they also reject them. This, however, is not all. Of the immense multitude of reprobates there shall be none who will not increase in others their pain by their horrible appearance, by their raging fury, by their frightful shrieks and groans.

4th. The damned having lost God, and with

God everything, fall into the power of the Devil. God lays aside all dominion over the damned and gives them over completely to the Devil. The Devil is a creature of extraordinary knowledge and power, of implacable hatred, fury and rage towards mankind. What have not the damned to fear from such a master?

AFFECTIONS.

Confession.—How dreadful are Thy judgments, O God! What an infinite evil then is sin, and how bitter are its fruits! To be eternally thrown off by Thee, to be eternally detested by Thy Elect, to be forever under the tyranny of Satan—such are the wages of sin! Have I until now believed this truth? Alas! this it is that increases my guilt; I have always believed that one sin is enough to lose God forever, and, with God all happiness; and yet I have sinned, and I have sinned without remorse, without fear, without terror.

Resolution.—What shall I do henceforth? On what do I resolve? I must behold Thee, O Sovereign Lord, in Thy glory, cost whatever it may. I must see and love Thee in Heaven, O Mary, my dearest mother, and you O Elect! should it cost me my life. To live and die without offending Thee, O God, by a single grievous sin is my resolve.

POINT II.

THE DAMNED HAVE IN GOD THEIR GREATEST ENEMY.

It is incontestible that they who lose God, their best friend, shall have him their greatest enemy. But how can God who is the Supreme Good and the only happiness of mortals, become their greatest evil? Duly weigh the effects of damnation and you will clearly understand this truth.

1st. The damned have a clear perception of God's infinite Beauty. Had the soul in Hell no greater knowledge of God than it had on earth, it would be free from its greatest torment; but the copious light it has when rid of the body, of the unspeakable happiness it could have enjoyed in God, renders its sorrow inconceivable.

2d. The damned have always before them the appearance of God in His wrath. "The Lord shall trouble them in His wrath." (Ps. xx. 10.) It is very difficult to understand how great this pain is. As the sight alone of the lovely countenance of God, enraptures all the Blessed, so the appearance alone of God in his anger fills all the damned with terror and despair.

3d. The damned shall live forever. The greatest desire of the damned is to die; for since they see that it is no longer possible to appease the anger of God, they wish for death, the only means to escape their misery. But it is in vain; as long as God lives, so long shall the damned live; and as He shall preserve the Elect forever to inebriate them with torrents of bliss, so shall He preserve the damned forever to overwhelm them with ceaseless agonies.

The unhappy reprobate shall curse their sins over and over; they shall shed enough tears to deluge the Earth; they shall burn for every mortal sin, millions and millions of years; and yet all these millions will not move God to pity; He continues to hate them and will hate them through a never ending Eternity. The damned, knowing this, always are in utter despair; they rave and yell in their fury and madness; their hatred for God becomes so intense that, as real devils they curse God, uttering against Him blasphemies without end, and loathing him so much, that, if they could, they would annihilate Him.

AFFECTIONS.

Fear.—O how delightful must it be to have before one's eyes a bountiful God, and how woeful to have a wrathful God! How sweet it is to experience the liberality of God and how bitter to fall into the hands of an avenging God! How consoling it will be to possess God eternally, and how heartrending to lose Him eternally! What can secure me from the infinite evil of Hell? Alas! my soul, thou hast sinned and for thee there is no other means of salvation than a true penance and amendment. Lamenting with all the powers of my soul, I turn then to Thee, O God!

Compunction.—I hate, detest, execrate with my whole heart, all the sins I have committed up to this moment. I see and acknowledge what an evil I have done. Sin is the greatest injury to Thee, because it is an offence against Thy infinite goodness and mercy. Sin is also the greatest injury to myself, because it is the ruin of my immortal soul. I have sinned mortally; I have lost Thee, O God, my last end and my only happiness, and I can recover Thee only by Thy grace, and by my own penance. Had I a thousand lives, I would willingly give them up, could I only revoke my sins. Supply, O Jesus, what is wanting to me, and in place of my sorrow I offer the sorrow which Thou, on account of my sins, hast felt in the Garden.

Resolution.—What shall I do henceforth? I will sin no more, O Jesus! I will rather choose death than sin, can I not avoid it in any other way. Imprint deeply, O Jesus, in my heart, this resolution, maintain it and grant that I may never swerve therefrom.

THIRD DAY

Meditation 4.

On the Second Pain of Hell, the Pain of the Senses.

POINT I.

The Pains of the Senses in Hell are Terrible in their Nature.

Represent to yourself Hell as a large prison in the centre of the Earth, and filled with a fire of sulphur and brimstone. Behold the damned lie in this prison, as close together as sheep in a pen (Ps. xlviii. 15).

Consider, now, what fire this is in which the damned burn:

1st. This fire is universal, burning the whole body and the whole soul.

The damned are in a place assigned to them by Divine Justice. As the fish in the ocean are surrounded by water, they are environed and thoroughly penetrated by this fire. Their heads, their eyes, their ears, cheeks, mouth, and lips are all fire; in short, the whole body is only fire. And, what is more horrible, this fire is in the memory, in the understanding, and in the will.

Were you in a furnace, so that one of your

arms would be in the fire and the rest of the body out of it, what inconceivable pain would you not feel? What must it then be to have, not only one arm, but all the senses and members of the body, as well as the faculties of the soul, encompassed and permeated by fire?

2d. This fire is much more terrible than we can imagine. How violent soever we may suppose fire on Earth to be, it is only a shadow of the fire of Hell. For the Justice of God uses it as an instrument to wreak vengeance on those who have here laughed to scorn His Supreme Majesty. He has given this fire, as it were, infinite power. The malice of sin is so great, that the fire of this Earth is not sufficient to punish it adequately. He imparts to the fire of Hell a power which no created intelligence can comprehend. And yet you, who shrink from the sufferings of an imaginary furnace, refuse slight sacrifices, petty humiliations, slight sufferings—in short, everything repugnant to the senses, though willed for you by an infinitely wise God, that you may not fall into the furnace heated by His anger—the everlasting flames of Hell.

AFFECTIONS.

Fear.—I have known and believed all these truths, O my God! But how have I lived? I have sinned; I have deserved Hell, and for what? Was it for a kingdom, or was I threatened with death? No! for a paltry gratification I have offended Thee. How blind, how foolish I was!

How cruel to myself! But I trust, O merciful God, that the past is forgiven. What frightens me is the future. I may sin again and die in my sins, and be damned forever. The vicious inclinations which ruined me are not yet uprooted; Divine Justice is not yet satisfied; my penance has been but trifling, and my weakness is evident, but Thy mercy is infinite.

A Prayer for Grace.—O my God! in such frightful uncertainty of my salvation, I lift up my hands and eyes to Thee, and humbly crave Thy mercy. My God and my Saviour! remember the wounds which Thou didst receive for me, and the blood which Thou didst shed for me. Remember the patience with which Thou hast tolerated my sinfulness so long, and the mercy with which Thou didst so tenderly invite me to repentance. Remember the benevolence with which Thou didst choose me for the religious state, in preference to many millions, and the love with which, notwithstanding the abuse of so many graces, Thou dost still spur me on to perfection. Shall, then, all this be lost on me? Yes, O my Saviour! it will be, unless Thou hast mercy on me, a wretched sinner.

POINT II.

The Pains of the Senses in Hell are Terrible in their Duration.

The damned lose God forever and burn in Hell forever. But what is Eternity? No angelic intellect can comprehend it, and how can you? Yet, in order that you may form some idea of it, consider the following truths:

1st. The pains of Hell are without end. This is the frightful truth which made the greatest Saints tremble. After the last day and the last judgment the damned shall plunge into Hell and "the gate shall be shut," never, no, never more, to be opened. Then shall pass away as many thousand years as there are leaves on trees, as many thousand years as there are drops of water in all the seas and oceans, as many thousand years as there are grains of sand on the Earth, and as many thousand years as there are atoms in the air. And, after the lapse of this tremendous number of years, there is Eternity yet! The one-half of it shall not have gone by, nor the hundredth part, nor the thousandth part, nor even a single part, compared with what shall remain. Again it begins, and shall last yet a hundred times—nay, a million times longer! After this almost infinite number of years, the half of Eternity is not yet gone by, not the hundredth part, not the millionth part—naught worth while shall as yet have passed away. And still, up to this supposed time, the damned shall have burned and shall burn over and over as many Eternities as there are still in infinity. They "shall be tormented for ever and ever" (Apoc. xx. 10). O mystery of all mysteries! O terror above all terrors! O Eternity! Who can understand thee?

Let us suppose Cain in Hell, shedding every thousand years only one tear. Cain would have now shed but five tears. What number of years must still elapse till Cain's thousandth-year tear will equal the drops of water in the deluge, which rose, as Scripture says, nearly twenty-seven feet above the highest mountains of the Earth? And yet, O incomprehensible truth! a time will come when his tears will deluge the whole world! And, after this, let us suppose God to dry up the waters, and Cain to begin again to weep. He would then weep another deluge—he would weep a hundred deluges—a thousand deluges; yet after all this the Eternity of the damned will have but begun to exist. It shall last as long as God will be God.

2d. The pains of Hell are without interruption and without alleviation. The damned are never to have any comfort, but always to suffer, to be hated forever by God and by His Elect, and to be cursed by Heaven and Hell forever and ever.

AFFECTIONS.

Thanksgiving.—O my God! I have a faint idea of what Eternity is; I now see what Hell is. It is a place of the most excruciating pains; a place of the utmost despair; a place which I have deserved by my sins, and in which I would now be, had not the infinite mercy of God spared me—had not the ever-pitying heart of Jesus loved me.

Compunction.—What has been my gratitude to God for such infinite goodness? I should have given Him my whole heart, loved Him with my whole soul—I should have worked for Him with all my strength and sought to please Him alone. I should have joyfully undergone all trials to prove to Him my love. But I have made little of Him, I have insulted Him, I have despised Him. My God, my God, I am an ungrateful wretch! I acknowledge and detest my ingratitude. O Jesus, take pity on me! I am more than ever resolved to die rather than to offend Thee once more.

Meditation 5.

WHAT FRUITS SHALL NOW BE GATHERED FROM THE PRECEDING MEDITATIONS?

Up to this time we have considered the evil of losing one's end by sin; but what good will this knowledge do us, if we reap no benefit from it?

THE FIRST FRUIT IS TO CONCEIVE A THOROUGH SORROW FOR OUR SINS.

What is the state of your conscience? Suppose an Angel to come from Heaven and to say to you: Settle all earthly concerns; in an hour you shall stand before your judge. Would you like to die in the state in which you now are? Have all your confessions been such as now to give you an assurance of the forgiveness of your sins? If not, see to it at once, and prepare to appear "before the judgment-seat of Christ." (2 Cor. v. 10.) For this purpose two resolutions are required:

1st. To make, during this retreat, after a reasonably strict examination of your conscience, and with due consideration of the motives of contrition, a confession so exact that your conscience may give you testimony of having done all that God requires of you to obtain pardon of your sins.

2d. Henceforth always to confess your sins in the same way; as if each confession were to be your last.

THE SECOND FRUIT IS TO SATISFY THE DIVINE JUSTICE AS MUCH AS POSSIBLE FOR PAST SINS.

Take another glance at Hell and imagine you hear God saying to one of the damned: I will show mercy to you on this condition: You must return to the world and silently suffer through love for Me, all the crosses and trials which I may send you, and then you will afterwards come unto Me in my Heavenly mansions. O blessed be forever Thy infinite Goodness, this reprobate would say, I joyfully undergo all that man has ever suffered, if Thou allow me to behold Thee in Thy glory. You who go through this meditation, have you not deserved Hell, and is not the time which God gave you in granting space for penance, a grace as great as if He had drawn you out of Hell? Why not, then, earnestly endeavor to do penance by patiently undergoing every adversity, in order to repair the injuries which you have done to God by your sins? Take, therefore, these resolutions:

1st. To use with all possible care and fervor the means which God ordains for the satisfaction of sin, which are: Frequent confession and communion; saying or hearing Mass; gaining of Indulgences; acts of perfect contrition and works of mortification.

2d. To bear patiently and cheerfully the trials and tribulations of your state of life; to discharge faithfully and exactly all its duties, remembering that what you now suffer is but trifling in comparison with the eternal pains of Hell.

THE THIRD FRUIT IS TO AVOID ALL VENIAL SINS, ESPECIALLY THOSE WHICH LEAD TO MORTAL SIN.

It suffices not to choose death in preference to mortal sin; we must also avoid venial sin. The person who is not at present thus disposed can have no sure hope of salvation. But to avoid venial sin we must as St. John Climacus says, "daily add, fire to fire, fervor to fervor, zeal to zeal."

To preserve ourselves in fervor, we must try to shun the following sins:

1st. Harboring suspicions, rash judgment, and contempt of others.

2d. Nourishing anger and indignation.

3d. Introducing into conversations the imperfections of others, and thus disturbing or perhaps destroying union and fraternal charity.

4th. Omitting through negligence the spiritual exercises, or performing them with voluntary distractions.

5th. Fostering in our hearts an inordinate affection for any one; giving knowingly and willingly occasion to impure thoughts, or being remiss in banishing them.

6th. Taking delight in one's self and one's actions.

7th. Receiving the sacraments through mere routine and without preparation.

8th. Suffering adversities and trials impatiently, not regarding them as coming from the beneficent hand of God.

9th. Purposely being gloomy and sullen, and not manifesting one's bad inclinations, weakness, and faults to those who should know them.

These are the sins of those who have not the spirit of religious life. If you do not resolve to shun those sins, you will not gather the least fruit from the exercises; nor will you ever arrive even at the lowest degree of perfection—you will never be in such a state as to expect death without fear. A traveller retraces his steps when he discovers that he has wandered from the right road. Let us then make up our minds to take the necessary steps to perfection, and express our resolve, with the crucifix in our hands, in the following manner:

O Jesus my Crucified Lord! I see what it is

to possess Thee forever. I understand what it is to lose Thee forever. O happy me if I find Thee! unhappy me if I lose Thee! I see that I never can securely hope for the former, and must always fear the latter, as long as I do not give myself up to Thee, without reserve and without delay.

I seek Thee, O my God, I sigh after Thee and wish to possess Thee. Thou art my end, my only happiness, and sole object of all my desires. O Jesus, by Thy precious blood, I humbly entreat Thee to strengthen my weakness, and to grant me the grace to carry out this my good purpose as long as life remains.

SECOND WEEK.

THE ILLUMINATIVE WAY.

The second week of the exercises comprises five meditations. During the first week we have mourned over our sins, and resolved to love God with our whole heart and to seek this our end with all our strength; but as we are blind and do not see the way that securely leads thereto, our Heavenly Father has given us His only begotten Son as a leader whom we have to follow, and as a model which we have to imitate.

Meditation 1.

ON THE REIGN OF CHRIST.

POINT I.

IT IS JUST TO FOLLOW CHRIST.

There are two points which clearly demonstrate how just it is. Consider them attentively.

1st. Our first parents fell away from God and deprived themselves and us of the right to Heaven. Of the many millions of men who have ever been and who shall ever be on earth, not one would have entered Heaven. What a misfortune that would be for mankind! Not one of them would have ever glorified God. What a loss for the glory of God! But Christ came, the gates of Heaven were again opened for all; and in consequence myriads of saints shall glorify His name forever. What can there be more just than that we follow our Lord and strive to gain so noble an end—the eternal glory of God and the everlasting happiness of man?

2d. The conditions on which Christ invites us are light. When earthly potentates have to perform a hard work, to face a danger, or to overcome a difficulty, they do not go personally, but send their subjects. But Christ acts otherwise. I do not wish, says He, those who follow me to have worse clothing or dwelling, worse food or drink, than I. I do not wish them to labor more than I. I do not wish them to suffer more than I. I do not wish them to go first, I will walk before them and show the way—all I require of them is to follow me. O what easy conditions these are! Jesus is innocent, and I am full of iniquities; Jesus is the Supreme Lord, and I a mere creature; Heaven belongs to Jesus, Hell to me, and yet Jesus does not wish me to labor or suffer more than He; He only wishes me to walk in His footsteps.

AFFECTIONS.

Thanksgiving.—If, in inviting me to follow Thee, O Jesus, Thou hadst no other end than the honor and glory of Thy Heavenly Father, it would be a sufficient reason, to hearken to Thy invitation. For I, Thy creature, would be bound to spend my whole life in Thy service. But no; Thy desire is not only the honor and glory of Thy Heavenly Father, but also my eternal salvation and happiness. Thou invitest me to follow Thee in order that I may share with Thee in Heaven the same glory and the same happiness. O what gratitude do not I then owe Thee!

Resolution.—O Jesus! to follow Thee is the work on which depends, not only the honor and glory of Thy Heavenly Father, but also my own salvation. I will follow Thee as closely as possible, in spite of nature, and with complete self-denial. I am a creature who has committed a multitude of sins, and therefore deserve Hell; how can I refuse then to do or to suffer what Thou, Innocence and Sanctity itself, my God and my Redeemer, hast done and suffered?

POINT II.

IT IS EASY TO FOLLOW CHRIST.

1st. On account of the peace of soul we experience, and the delight we feel in serving God.

Christ was not always in afflictions. He had joys also. In His nativity men banished Him to a bleak stable, but Angels descended from Heaven to proclaim His glory. In the desert the Devil tempted Him, but Angels came and ministered unto Him. In His public life, whilst He gave forth the words of life, He was calumniated and persecuted; but on Mount Thabor He was transfigured and appeared in His glory; not to speak of the inexplicable delights which, by reason of the hypostatic union, His soul felt.

Since the life of our Lord was not a continual cross, yours will not be such, because He says expressly: I do not wish you to suffer more than I suffered. Assuredly, the more perfectly you follow Christ, the greater will be your consolations, interior joy, and happiness. Hear His own words: " My yoke is sweet and my burden is light." To be near Jesus is always sweet, even in the midst of adversities; to be far from Jesus is always bitter, even in the midst of joys. If any consolation is given here below, the one who faithfully follows Christ shall certainly have this consolation. " What can the world profit thee without Jesus? To be without Jesus is a grievous Hell, and to be with Jesus a sweet Paradise" (The Following of Christ, ii. 8, 2).

2d. On account of the immense glory and boundless treasures of rewards which He stores up for them in the next life. After some years you shall be in Heaven; how full of comfort this thought is—how full of sweetness in all trials! Imagine you see your Divine Redeemer carrying a heavy cross, earnestly looking at you at the same time, whilst you behold in Heaven the royal throne prepared for you above many millions of the Elect, and you hear Him addressing you thus: Lo! this throne is yours; you shall possess it forever if you follow Me closely for a short time. Would you not then follow Him with great joy? Would not these words console you in all your labors and afflictions? Why cannot faith do as much as this sight does? Faith teaches you that, if you follow Christ, a Heavenly crown awaits you, which shall be yours forever.

AFFECTIONS.

Hope and Confidence.—I believe, O Jesus! that Thy yoke is sweet and Thy burden light. For these are Thy words; Thou hast spoken them, who hast never deceived and never shall deceive. My self-love and my cowardice alone make the following of Thee difficult; could I but overcome myself courageously and walk in Thy footsteps for a few years, I would soon experience how true these Thy words are. According to the world's notions, what a miserable life these tender virgins seem to lead who withdraw into convents! Nevertheless, they find no sweetness but in God's service. How wretched, in the estimation of the same world, are they who are persecuted, oppressed, calumniated, and despised? And yet they receive from our Lord the most wonderful communication of grace. Shall I, then, be the only one to whom He will never give any Heavenly comfort? Shall I be the only one whom He will never allow to taste His consolation? No! Jesus, I hope and confide in Thy mercy, that Thou wilt grant me the grace which shall make the following of Thee easy.

POINT III.

IT IS NECESSARY TO FOLLOW CHRIST.

I suppose you desire to tend to perfection. For this it is absolutely necessary that you follow Christ in everything as closely as possible. "If thou wilt be perfect," said our Saviour, "come, follow me." Do you understand this truth? Alas! the knowledge is not wanting; the road on which Christ walked is too rough. It terrifies you; but this is the very thing that is required.

1st. Christ is Infinite Wisdom and Truth. He has come into this world to show the road to sanctity. Were there a more certain and a better way to it than the one which He marked out, He would not have been Infinite Wisdom, because He ignored this way; nor Infinite Truth, because He would have deceived us. But it would be blasphemy to assert either.

2d. God is Infinite Love and Goodness.

God loves man, and, without a good reason, He cannot inflict sufferings and torments. Hence it follows that could an agreeable path equally conduct us to sanctity as a rough, narrow, and painful one, His love for us would not have selected the more difficult one. He, in His prevision of the future, saw that a path agreeable to the senses and pleasing to nature would lead us to our eternal perdition; for this reason He assigned us the rougher path, walked in it Himself, and invited us to follow Him.

Pause here and say to yourself: In this world I must choose between the two places of the next; one, Hell, is infinitely miserable, the other, Heaven, infinitely blissful. To these two places only two roads lead—a broad one, on which numberless human beings walk, conducts to Hell; a rough and narrow road, on which Christ, with a small number of His Elect, walks, leads to Heaven. On which of the two have I hitherto gone, and which shall I choose for the future?

AFFECTIONS.

Compunction.—The retrospective view of my past life shows that, although I have acknowledged Thee, O Jesus! as my God and my Redeemer, I have not followed Thee as my Leader. These virtues, which Thou calledst a sweet yoke and a light burden, I deemed too heavy a load for my weakness. I detracted from Thy Wisdom, as if Thou knewest not what I could bear; and I disparaged Thy Goodness, as if Thou didst impose too much on me. O my God and my Redeemer! my Master and Leader! I recognize my mistake, I see my wickedness, and I detest it with all my heart. Oh! how happy would I be at this moment had I always walked on the road on which Thou didst walk!

An Act of Self-Offering.—But how long shall this last? Thou art the Way, the Truth, and the Life. I give myself up to Thee, O my blessed Saviour! with my whole heart, and without reserve. I shall tread in Thy footsteps. Go, therefore, before me and lead me. Lead me through contempt and humiliations, through calumnies and persecutions, and I will still follow Thee. Lead me through pains and afflictions, and I will not cease to follow Thee. Lead me through self-denial and self-annihilation, and I will continue to follow Thee. Where Thou art, O Jesus! my life, I will also be. What Thou dost I will also do; what Thou didst suffer I will also suffer. Only give me Thy grace, and I ask no more

FOURTH DAY.

Meditation 2.

ON THE WONDERFUL HUMILITY WHICH CHRIST EXHIBITED IN HIS INCARNATION AND HIS BIRTH.

POINT I.

CHRIST IN HIS INCARNATION AND BIRTH UTTERLY DEBASED HIMSELF.

How many astonishing acts of self-abasement appear therein?

1st. He took upon Himself human nature. Were your faith enlightened you could not sufficiently admire this self-abasement. A comparison may help to illustrate it. There was once a king having absolute power, immense riches, and exceedingly great wisdom and all princely virtues; the nobility, the army, the people loved him as a father; nothing was wanting to complete his happiness. This great monarch secretly doffed his royal garments, donned a beggar's clothes, left the country, became a servant to a farmer in a foreign land, and remained unknown in this humble service till death. This was indeed an inconceivable abasement!

Let us look with the eyes of faith on the lovely Infant in the crib at Bethlehem. Who is He? The Lord of the world, the Creator of Heaven and Earth; to whom the whole universe, with all its riches and treasures, belongs. Notwithstanding His infinite excellence and happiness He quitted Heaven, where he was adored by all the Angels; He took up His abode on Earth; He became a man of sorrows and infirmities and remained in this state till death. Can any human understanding conceive self-abasement like unto this?

2d. He took upon Himself human nature as an Infant. Is there anything more helpless than an infant? It can neither stand nor walk, but it must always be assisted and carried by another. It cannot speak, and can only manifest its needs by crying. We, when infants, could well undergo this, because we had no consciousness, but Christ, who was Infinite Wisdom, felt the entire helplessness of this condition. He could have come into this world in the bloom of manhood, but he willed it not; He came as a little child, that He might humble Himself the more and teach us humility the better.

Imagine you see the Divine Infant lying in the manger. Infant though He is, He is nevertheless God who created Heaven and Earth. He is the Word of God and He cannot speak a word. He is God, infinitely rich, before whom all earthly sovereigns are mere beggars; and he has no other dwelling than a wretched stable.

AFFECTIONS.

Confusion.—O most humble Jesus, how different are the desires of my heart from Thine! Thou debasest Thyself, and I exalt myself, with Lucifer, to the highest Heaven. Thou bringest Thyself down to the feeble state of an infant, and I always desire a position more and more honorable in the sight of men. Thou hidest Thyself and all the excellences which thou possessest, that no praise may be given Thee; and I desire the good which is in me to be seen that I may be praised the more—in short, all Thy thoughts are for lowliness and self-abasement, and mine for self-exaltation and worldly honor. Alas! I acknowledge it. O Jesus, I have not yet Thy spirit, and my views are as distant from Thine as Earth is from Heaven.

Compunction.—I see and confess, O Jesus, that I have erred; this is not the path in which Thou didst walk. I am sorry for all my vain thoughts and desires, for all the boastful words which I have ever spoken, for all the vain-glorious deeds which I have ever performed. To me therefore confusion and contempt are justly due; but to Thee praise, honor, and glory.

Following of Christ, iii. B., Chaps. xli, xlii.

POINT II.

CHRIST, FROM HIS BIRTH AND ALL THROUGH LIFE, WILLINGLY SUBMITTED TO ALL THE HUMILIATIONS WHICH CAME UPON HIM FROM OTHERS.

1st. How did the world receive Him in His birth? What greater affront could be offered to a man than to be so far rejected that not one of his kindred would give him shelter for one night? This happened to Christ in the town of Bethlehem. Young and old, rich and poor, found in it a lodging. Jesus alone, with His blessed Mother, was everywhere refused admittance. He first beholds the light in a stable. How did He submit to it? With joy. He Himself willed it, for if He had willed the contrary, He would have sent before Him hosts of Angels to announce His coming; He might on entering the town have made the Earth tremble; He might have sent thunder and lightning to terrify its inhabitants and make them adore His Majesty.

2d. How has the world treated Him after His birth? It treated Him worse than at His birth. A new star had appeared in the heavens; the wise men had come from the East and announced His birth. One would think that all Jerusalem would run flocking out of their houses to adore the Infant Jesus. O fearful ingratitude! Out of so many hundred thousands not one was found to take a step to see Jesus. Even their king sought to kill Him; the time was chosen and the Child Jesus had to flee from His own country to escape death.

3d. What did the world think of Christ after He had grown up? It thought no more of Him than it did at His birth. He lived with His parents at Nazareth, His occupation was to work at home with His Foster-Father and to earn His daily bread in the sweat of His brow. No one imagined that Joseph's son was a Man-God; the Heavenly Father kept the secret and gave no sign that Jesus of Nazareth was His beloved Son. Mary and Joseph revealed it not and Jesus Himself hid from the eyes of men all the treasures of His human and divine nature. The God-Man, who had created Heaven and Earth, passed in the eyes of the world as a carpenter's son.

AFFECTIONS.

Contempt of One's Self.—How little didst Thou, O Saviour, think of honor and esteem, and how precious in Thy sight was contempt! What a lesson is this for me! Thou fleest honor, and I flee contempt; Thou seekest to be unknown, and I seek to be known and even admired; Thou didst take pleasure in being despised, and I in being praised and esteemed. If Thy spirit is the road to sanctity, mine is the way to perdition. If Thy humility is the road to Heaven, my pride is the way to Hell.

Acknowledgment —True, I am far more esteemed than Thou wast, and yet I am not satisfied; I am honored and treated with reverence for being a religious; but when wast Thou honored? The will of my Heavenly Father, my progress in virtue, the sanctity of my soul, must yield to this my pride. This is a wound which only Thou, O God, canst heal.

POINT III.

Considerations on the Humility of Jesus Christ.

You have now before you one of the principal points of the spiritual life; ask Divine light and help to reflect on it attentively.

1st. Nothing is more agreeable to God than a soul that has a love for contempt and self-annihilation. Let us suppose we had lived before the coming of Christ, and that our Heavenly Father had asked us in what manner He should send His Son into the world, what would we have answered? We would, no doubt, have said, His foster-father must be a monarch, His mother a queen, His dwelling a magnificent palace; angels must announce His coming, the people must assemble and adore the new-born God. Thus we would have thought and said. Yet God the Father willed the parents of His beloved Son to be poor, the place of His birth to be a stable, His dwelling a poor home at Nazareth, His life to be hidden, and His death to be that of a malefactor, in the midst of insults and torments. How blind we are! We love, above all, the esteem and applause of the world; Jesus loves nothing so much as contempt and self-annihilation. What else do you see in Him but humiliations and torture? And yet this was the sacrifice that pleased His Heavenly Father and procured the salvation of mankind.

2d. God hates nothing so much in a soul as the love of honor and esteem. The less conformity a soul has with Jesus Christ the less it is esteemed by God the Father. But what conformity with Jesus Christ can a soul have that loves the praise and esteem of men? Jesus rejoiced only in injuries; the life of Jesus commenced and ended with outrages. Compare yourself with Jesus; and see what there is in you like unto Him.

AFFECTIONS.

Confession and Sorrow.—In Thy heart, O Jesus, is extreme horror of all vainglory, and the most ardent desire of contempt and of affronts, and in my heart just the contrary—the greatest horror of contempt and of affronts, and the greatest satisfaction in vainglory. What increases my misery is, that I refuse the medicine, and when I am compelled to take it, it proves hurtful to me. The surest and best means to root out pride would be confusion, contempt and calumny; but I, unhappy mortal, love my misfortune; I cherish my pride and reject humiliation. Through Thy mercy I have to-day received the grace to see and to hate my misery. What have I to glory in, or why do I desire to be esteemed? Truly vainglory is an evil plague, a very great vanity, because it draws us away from true glory and robs us of heavenly grace; for whilst a man takes complacency in himself, he displeases Thee; whilst he seeks after the praises of men, he is deprived of true virtues. (The Following of Christ, iii. B., Chap. xl., 4.)

Resolutions and Supplication.—To-day I ask of Thee, O Jesus, the virtue of humility. It is the indication of Thy spirit, the distinguishing mark of Thy true followers, and the way to intimate union with Thee. A proud soul can never enter into familiar friendship with Thee, because it is an abomination before Thee. Should I not take all pains to acquire the virtue of humility?

I firmly purpose then, O Jesus, first, never willingly to acquiesce in any vain thought, or in any self-complacency, not to speak a word in my own praise, and never through vanity to do any work. Second, joyfully to accept all contempt from whatever source it may come, and bear it silently. O Jesus, how easy it is to make these resolutions, but how difficult to carry them out! Thou, O Jesus, art my hope and my strength!

Meditation 3.

ON THE WONDERFUL OBEDIENCE OF CHRIST IN HIS HIDDEN LIFE.

POINT I.

JESUS UNDERWENT, FOR THE LOVE OF HIS HEAVENLY FATHER AND FOR ME, ALL THE HARDSHIPS WHICH PERFECT OBEDIENCE INVARIABLY BRINGS ON.

To give up one's own will, and to live until death according to the will of another, has many difficulties.

The first difficulty of obedience is that of the employments of our state of life. We often think the office with which the Superior charges us is too low for us. We believe that those who are preferred to us have less talent, and that we are endowed with all the capacity requisite for their office; and, in short, for any office. Your office is too low? Let us cast our eyes on Jesus. Who is He? The King of kings, the Lord of lords, the Supreme Ruler of Heaven and earth. What office has He? O wonder of wonders! Up to His thirtieth year He works at home, and obeys every order of His foster-father. Look at Him and consider the Divine Artisan, and if shame does not prevent you, you may complain of your office.

The second difficulty of obedience is the Su-

-perior who governs us. During the years of our religious life we have now and then Superiors whose government is severe and troublesome. Some are wanting in humility, and are too partial to those they like; others do not care to know the temper of their subjects, and treat them without consideration; some are deficient in charity, and have not much compassion on those under them; some lack meekness, and have not the necessary affability to win hearts and make the yoke of obedience sweet. They who desire to have true obedience must be like unto Jesus Christ, their model. He stands before Pilate's tribunal. The sentence is pronounced: He is condemned to death. How little would it have cost Him to free Himself from this condemnation! He could have shown to the whole world the injustice of this sentence. He could have hurled Pilate from his judgment-seat into hell. He could, as He did at another time, have escaped by making Himself invisible. Jesus does nothing of the kind. He receives the sentence from Pilate as if it came from His Heavenly Father. He obeys Him until death; yea, the death of the Cross. Who among you, then, can complain of your superiors, since Christ obeyed a most unjust judge?

3. Let us consider all the other difficulties of obedience. In religious life many things are commanded which are not agreeable to our taste. We consider them neither necessary, nor useful, nor becoming. We are ordered to do many

things to which we naturally feel a repugnance. Many things are enjoined which do not tally with our will, and which are by their nature troublesome, especially if they last very long. What did Christ do to set us an example, and to merit for us the grace to follow Him? Was it easy for Him to remain so many years in a workshop, and always to obey his foster-father's call? Was it easy for him to travel for three years from town to town, and to be ill treated in almost every place? Was it not painful for Him to hear the sentence of death passed on Him, and afterwards to die on an infamous cross? In all these difficulties Jesus Christ instantly obeyed, without a murmur; He obeyed with the most perfect resignation. Alas! what is our obedience compared with His?

AFFECTIONS.

Self-abasement.—In whatever way I look at my soul, I see, O Jesus, nothing conformable to Thee. I should entirely lay aside my own will and behold naught but Thee in my Superiors, observe their very looks, and not only not take their commands ill, but fulfil them joyfully. Thus should I obey. My vow of obedience, and the example which Thou gavest to me, demand this. But alas! how often have I failed in this respect by the obstinacy of my judgment, and by the stubbornness of my will. How many sins have I committed by my inward murmurs and my open complaints! Would not these sins, even if I had no others, be enough to cause me to fear Thy justice?

Compunction.—I acknowledge my infidelity, and detest it with all my heart. How great are these sins in Thy sight, and yet they seemed to me, until now, insignificant! As I have vowed obedience not to man, but to Thee, my God, so, by my disobedience, I have not offended man, but Thy supreme majesty. As often as I have preferred my judgment to the judgment of my superiors, I have despised Thy infinite wisdom. As often as I have resisted the will of my Superiors, I have set at naught Thy will. As often as I have censured in my heart, or with my tongue, the appointments of my Superiors, I have blamed the appointments of Thy infinite love and goodness. "He that heareth you heareth Me, and he that despiseth you despiseth Me." These are Thy words, O Jesus, and by them I see how guilty I am, and how blind I have been.

POINT II.

On the Wonderful Happiness of a Soul that practises Blind, and therefore Perfect, Obedience.

We have viewed attentively the obedience of Christ, let us now consider the happiness it gives.

1st. Those who are obedient know that they do the will of God at every moment. Let us imagine God permits your guardian angel to be seen by you day and night, to make known to you in every circumstance that which God requires. Could there be on earth a greater happiness? But lively faith will show that those who practise blind obedience are at every instant as much assured of the will of God as if an angel made it known to them. They are as certain of the will of God as Christ was at Nazareth. They have as much security of the will of God as had the Apostles, who heard the very words of life.

2d. All the works of those who are obedient become highly valuable and meritorious in the sight of God. Nothing is more wonderful than the value of obedience, for the smallest works done through obedience are very great before God. To eat and drink moderately out of obedience is a great work before God. To fast a whole year on bread and water without obedience is nothing before Him. To travel through the whole world and to preach everywhere the gospel without obedience is nothing before God; but to wash dishes or sweep a room out of obedience is a great work before Him. The only sure rule to measure the excellence of a work is the will of God. Return once more unto the workshop at Nazareth and contemplate Jesus. The labor which He did, low though it may appear, was so great that He, God-man that He was, could do no greater. Why so? Because it was the will of God, His Father.

3d. All who are obedient reach perfect sanctity in a short time. The two reasons are:

1. The nature of perfection and sanctity itself. To be holy is to do nothing else but the will of God and live as He wills. The obedient desire nothing, seek nothing, do nothing but what God wills. They rise at a time that God wills, go to bed when God wills, and pray when God wills; they therefore become holy in a short time.

2. The providence of God. God loves an obedient soul. He carries it in the bosom of His providence, as a mother carries her child in her arms. He governs and leads it, and takes care of all that concerns it. All Hell and earth may rise up against it; men may seek to check its onward course. It is in vain. This soul is under the protection of an infinitely wise, powerful and benevolent God. He will infallibly conduct it to the degree of sanctity which He wills for it, and bring it to Heaven to the throne of glory to which from eternity it was predestined.

AFFECTIONS.

Faith.—The Superiors rule, not in their own name, but in the name of Jesus Christ; they command, not in virtue of their own powers, but in the virtue of the power of Jesus Christ. Whatever they order I should approve and perform, not because it is their will, but that of Jesus Christ. Whoever believes this not should hearken to Christ's own words: "He that heareth you heareth Me, and he that despiseth you despiseth Me" (St. Luke, x. 16). This, Thy saying, O Jesus, I humbly accept. I believe that the will of my Superiors is Thy will; I believe that their appointments are Thine, and their commands Thine. I believe that I cannot withdraw myself from their guidance and direction without withdrawing myself from the guidance and direction of Thy providence.

Hope and Confidence.—I have vowed obedience, therefore I gave over to Thee my will and my liberty forever, and Thou didst promise to guide and govern me through my Superiors. I commit myself to Thy providence, and will live henceforth without further temporal care and trouble. Thou art Infinite Wisdom, and knowest what offices are the best for me. Thou art Infinite Goodness, and wilt take care that my Superiors give only such commands as are for my greatest good. Thou art Infinite Truth, and didst pledge Thy word that they who hear Superiors hear Thee.

AN ACT OF LOVE AND SELF-OFFERING.

Animated with confidence, O Jesus, my only and Supreme Good, I throw myself down into the abyss of my nothingness. This moment I promise and vow a new obedience; I renounce my judgment, my will, my liberty, and give them entirely and perfectly up to those whom Thou didst appoint to guide and govern me.

Meditation 4.

ON THE WONDERFUL CHARITY AND MEEKNESS OF CHRIST IN HIS PUBLIC LIFE.

POINT I.

CHRIST UNDERWENT FIRST THE HARDSHIPS WHICH RENDER CHARITY AND MEEKNESS DIFFICULT.

These two virtues are essential to sanctity. Let us look at the example of Christ, and resolve to bear what He has borne for us. Here are the hardships of these two virtues:

1st. To have to deal with men on whom all our pains and labors are lost. What did not Christ do to convert the Jews? For three years He travelled over Judea and Samaria. He went from town to town and preached with Divine eloquence. He heaped upon them all sorts of blessings, He wrought many miracles, and invited them so lovingly to His Kingdom. But what did it avail? Some despised Him and said, Where has the son of a carpenter learned these things? Others laughed at Him and derided His doctrine. The Pharisees called Him a wicked man who keeps not the law. The highpriest publicly condemned His doctrine, and exhorted the people not to be seduced by Him, and excommunicated those who followed Him.

Hence but few were converted; the rest remained obstinate and inflexible. How hard it is to love people of this sort.

2d. To have to deal with persons, who, through envy and hatred, interpret everything wrongly. Almost at every step of His public life Christ encountered this hardship. Through love and compassion He often cured the sick on the Sabbath. Impious men said: He cannot be from God because He keeps not the Sabbath day. He dined with public sinners that He might convert them; they said: He is a wine-bibber and loves good cheer. He wrought many wonders to bring men to the knowledge of God; they said: He works not the miracles by Himself, but the Devil works them through Him.

3d. To have to deal with people who acknowledge no benefit and only return evil for good. Jesus came to Nazareth, preached in the synagogue, and showed His fellow-citizens all imaginable love. What was their gratitude for this grace? They led Him to a rock to throw Him down. He preached at Jerusalem, and told them that He was the Son of God and the promised Messiah. They called Him a blasphemer, and wished to stone Him to death.

4th. To have around one's self false brethren. Jesus knew what lay hidden in Judas's heart. He knew that he was the one who after some time would betray Him and deliver Him up to death.

5th. To have to deal with people who, as we

Christ's Wonderful Charity and Meekness.

know, actually abhor and detest us. The high-priests and Scribes in their secret councils condemned Jesus to death; they declared publicly that they would exclude from the synagogue those who followed Him. They issued an order to apprehend Christ as an impostor and to deliver Him into their hands; nevertheless He loved them and He loved them most tenderly with a father's love.

AFFECTIONS.

Confusion.—How strong and ardent is Thy love, O Jesus, how weak and cold is mine! Thou hadst to converse with people who openly reproached and abused Thee; who everywhere proclaimed Thee an impostor and blasphemer; who under the mask of friendship sought to deliver Thee up to Thy enemies; who resolved not to cease until they had nailed Thee on the Cross. What injurious treatment was this! But it could not extinguish Thy love. Ah! woe is me! How little have I of Thy meekness and Thy love! A severe look, a contemptuous word, an unkind refusal suffices to smother my charity. This is the progress I have made after Thy many graces!

Resolution.—O Jesus, shall this be always so? Shall my heart always remain tepid and cold? Shall I never have charity and meekness? Thou didst call me, O Jesus, to a religious life to follow Thee as closely as possible; it was the first lesson Thou hast taught mankind: " Learn of me, because I am meek and humble of heart." How shall I dare to appear before Thee, if I have not these virtues? What account shall I give to Thee of the abuse of so many graces?

POINT II.

THE MARVELLOUS QUALITIES OF JESUS'S CHARITY FOR US.

1st. His charity, notwithstanding the many injuries inflicted on Him, was ever ardent. This indeed was truly wonderful, for Jesus was Omniscience itself; He saw in the days of His life many who hated Him, who asserted that He was an impostor, who insulted and blasphemed Him, and sought to condemn Him to the death of the Cross; all this He saw, and always loved most ardently. How would you feel if surrounded by hundreds of thousands who supposed you to be wicked, who wherever they went slandered you, and even sought to take your life?

2d. His charity, notwithstanding the many insults offered to Him, was always tender. For three years He saw Judas, He knew his evil intention, but this diminished not His love; He conversed with him, and treated him as affably as He did the rest of the Apostles. He gave both him and them power to work miracles; at the Last Supper He washed his feet like those of the others, so that even the Apostles suspected nothing. Yea, even at the moment when he betrayed Him into the hands of His enemies, He called him *friend* and kissed him. Could He have conversed more lovingly with St. John, whom He loved best of all the Apostles?

3d. His charity, notwithstanding the many affronts heaped upon Him, was constantly beneficent and generous. While the daily ingratitude of the Jews towards Him increased in rage and fury, He multiplied the more His benefits towards them. He prayed continually with all the fervor of His heart to His Heavenly Father for their salvation. Not a week passed without His working miracles and performing prodigies to bring them to the knowledge of God. Malchus was one of those who had come to apprehend Jesus, and whose ear was cut off; Jesus but stretched forth His hand and healed his ear.

AFFECTIONS.

Compunction.—Now I know, O Jesus, what it is to love. To love those who love us, who are well disposed towards us, who do us good, is to love as the Jews and heathens. To love those who are not well disposed towards us, who wrong and calumniate us, is to love as Jesus did. But how have I loved? Alas! how feeble is my love! My love most of the time has been that of the Jews and heathens. Seldom have I loved as Jesus loved. I have erred then, and I have not the virtue which is the essential feature of Christianity, the apple of the eye of a religious community and the groundwork of perfection. I detest, O Jesus, with my whole heart everything which I have done against this amiable virtue, and I humbly crave Thy pardon.

Love.—Henceforth my first care and my earnest endeavor shall be to love God with my whole heart, and for His sake my neighbor as myself. These are the two precepts which, O my Saviour, Thou hast taught and shown by Thy example. Thou didst die for all, and hast commanded me to love all; I will love them, therefore, and love them as myself. Thou, O Jesus, have mercy on them, and give every one of them as much temporal and eternal happiness as I wish for myself.

Resolution.—Such is the sentiment of my heart, but it is not sufficient, it must manifest itself in action—otherwise it is no love. What, then, will I do for the love of my neighbor? I will do that which I would like to be done to myself. I wish every one to have a good opinion of me; I will act thus towards others; no more suspicious, rash judgments or contempt on my part. I wish every one to treat me kindly; I will do the same for others. I wish every one to bear patiently with my faults and imperfections and not to speak ill of me; thus also will I act towards my neighbor. This is genuine and practical love. Grant me, O Jesus, the grace to love henceforth as Thou didst love.

FIFTH DAY.

Meditation 5.

THE CONCLUSION OF THE SECOND WEEK.

We have contemplated the pre-eminent virtues of Jesus Christ. Weigh now in your mind some of the maxims of the spiritual life.

1st. As much as you have of the spirit of Christ, so much have you of true sancity and perfection. If you desire to know what progress you have made on the road to perfection, see how much you have of this spirit. If everything in you corresponds with Christ's spirit, then you truly possess sanctity. The greater your resemblance to this model, the holier and more perfect you are.

2d. You have as much of the spirit of Christ as you have of His obedience, humility, meekness and charity. There is no virtue which in the life of Christ did not shine most perfectly; nevertheless He has not given such striking examples in the others as in these four virtues. The two last he enjoined on us as earnestly as if they comprised the very essence of His spirit. "Learn of Me," He said, "because I am meek and humble of heart." (St. Matt. xi. 29.)

3d. Hence you see the reason why so few,

even of the most strict religious orders of the Church, arrive at sanctity. The most of the religious are satisfied if they perform the exercises which are not painful to human nature. They meditate and pray, they do their works with a good intention, fulfil all the duties of their offices, and practise austerities according to their different rules But to cast off actively their own will, to be perfectly indifferent so as to be ready to do the bidding of the superiors at their beck, to repress the love of honor and willingly to accept contempt, gradually to overcome impatience and all feelings of indignation, to treat ill-natured and obstinate persons benignantly and affably, and to crush self-love completely—these are virtues which but few practise. The first means towards the attainment of perfection is purity of heart; we must devote our care to the purifying of our whole heart, because there lies the root of all our evils. When the heart is thoroughly cleansed, God fills the soul and all its powers, the memory, the understanding, and the will with His holy presence and love. This purity of heart leads to union with God, and no one attains thereto by any other means. Jesus does not communicate Himself to religious who do not strive after purity of heart; He lets them live and die in their inferiority. If then you earnestly seek sanctity and union with God, it is absolutely necessary that you walk in the footsteps of Christ and try to imitate His virtues.

Exercise of Obedience.

(1.) I will keep myself in continual indifference with respect to the behests of Superiors; consequently I will ask nothing, seek nothing, refuse nothing.

(2.) I will in all circumstances behold God in them, firmly believing that their will is God's will.

(3.) I will execute all their commands with reverence and exactness.

Exercise of Humility.

(1.) I will relinquish all love of honor so as to spurn all self-esteem or self-complacency; and I will never say a word or do the least action through vainglory.

(2.) I will leave my good name entirely to God, so as to bear contempt as often as it pleases His Divine Majesty.

(3.) I will accept with an undisturbed mind every humiliation from whatever source it may come.

Exercise of Meekness and Charity.

(1.) I will keep a benevolent heart for all mankind so as never willingly and knowingly to conceive angry feelings for any one.

(2.) In every circumstance I will treat all charitably and kindly.

(3.) Whatever may be done to me by others, I will suffer it silently, so as to return good for evil.

These are the points in which the spirit of Christ and the imitation of His virtues manifest themselves. Are you resolved to follow Jesus Christ? If so, offer yourself up to Him thus: Thy spirit, O Jesus, is to despise honor and to love contempt; to renounce my will and to follow that of others; to converse with all affably, and to suffer silently all reproaches and insults. Not only this is Thy spirit, but it is also the only way which leads to Thy love and to union with Thee. Thou art sanctity itself, and Thou canst never dwell in a heart unless it be cleansed from evil affections and be resplendent with Thy virtues. Oh, what ardent love for Thee, what familiar communication, what intimate union with Thee would I now have, had I died to myself and lived according to Thy spirit! O unhappy me, of what heavenly treasures have I deprived myself! But all is not yet lost! Through Thy mercy I know now Thy spirit and also the road which leads to Thee. I can yet cleanse my heart from all defilement; I can yet arrive at familiar communication and intimate union with Thee, I, O Jesus, who have so often offended Thee; I, who have abused so many graces; I, who for so many years have turned a deaf ear to Thy invitations.

THIRD WEEK.

Intermediate Meditation 1.

The Intermediate Meditations join more closely action with suffering.

THE TWO STANDARDS.

To understand well the purpose of this week, we must know that to follow Christ, to live according to His spirit, and to practise virtue as He practised it, cannot be done without suffering with courageous and generous spirit; for this reason our holy father Ignatius presents to us the example of Christ, that we may not refuse to suffer for God what He has suffered for us. The present Meditation, therefore, is directed towards this point, that we resolve earnestly to follow Christ and to live according to His spirit, cost what it may.

POINT I.

WHOM WE ARE TO FOLLOW—JESUS CHRIST OR SATAN—MAY BE SEEN FROM THE DESIGN OF THE TWO LEADERS WHOM WE NOW PROPOSE.

1st. The design of Jesus Christ is to draw all mortals to follow Him, that they may save their souls and eternally love and praise His Heavenly Father. The reason of this is the two-fold love which burns in His heart. The first is the tenderest love for His Heavenly Father; for as He loves Him most perfectly, He also desires that He may be forever praised, honored, glorified by men. The second is the most affectionate love for them; since He loves them most ardently, He wishes them to seek their salvation and to enjoy forever with Him His own bliss.

2d. The design of Satan is to draw all mortals to his standard, that thus they may desert and dishonor God and precipitate themselves into eternal perdition. He is fired with a two-fold hatred. First, hatred for God; for since he was cast out of Heaven by a just judgment, he intensely hates God, and cannot bear to see Him honored, praised and loved. Second, hatred for us; for as he knows the infinite glory and happiness prepared by God for us in Heaven, his hatred, envy and fury are savagely fierce; he employs every possible means to deprive us of this happiness and to drag us into his own misery. What choice will you now make? Which of the two leaders will you follow?

When the young Tobias was about to set out for a strange country, the Archangel Raphael offered himself, under the form of a young man, as guide. But let us suppose two young men had presented themselves as guides, one of whom was the Archangel and the other Satan, and that Tobias had rejected Raphael and had selected Satan; would he not have been a great fool to act so unwisely? You, like Tobias, are on a long journey and on a strange road, the road to eternity. Jesus and the Devil offer themselves as guides. Which of the two will you follow?

AFFECTIONS.

What a strange choice this is between Jesus and the Devil! Jesus is the only begotten Son of the Heavenly Father; Jesus is sanctity itself; Jesus seeks only my happiness. The Devil is the greatest enemy of God, a damned spirit; he hates me bitterly, he seeks nothing but my eternal perdition. What shall I do? I am ashamed to ask this question. Have I lost my senses to leave God and follow Satan? Do I hate myself so much as to turn away from the road to Heaven, and to rush madly to Hell? God forbid! Thou, O Jesus, art the way, the truth and the life. Thou art the Way which securely leads to bliss; the Truth which knows all dangers; the Life by which we shall possess eternal life. Receive me, O Jesus, under Thy standard. I will follow Thee and Thee alone till death.

POINT II.

WHOM WE ARE TO FOLLOW—JESUS CHRIST OR SATAN—MAY BE SEEN BY THE ENDS TO WHICH BOTH LEAD.

There is an infinite difference between the standard of Jesus Christ and that of Satan. Consider both well.

1st. Under the standard of Jesus we are invited to that which is hard and bitter to nature; viz., to voluntary poverty, to blind obedience, to continual self-abnegation, to humility and the love of contempt, to silence in trials and persecution, to joy in pains and tribulations. This is the spirit of Jesus Christ. But although such a life seems to be bitter, the end to which it leads is sweet and desirable. What is this end? It may be told in a few words, but you must reflect on them during your whole life. The end to which Jesus leads, is the avoidance of an infinite evil, namely, Hell—and the acquisition of an infinite good, which is — Heaven — and both for eternity.

2d. Under Satan's standard we are invited to that which is pleasing to nature. He promises those who follow him temporal goods and riches, the honor, the love and the esteem of men, the pleasures of the body, joyful, independent and unrestrained lives. This is the spirit of Satan. But what is the end to which this cunning and this accursed spirit leads? Ah! Be not deceived! The end is the loss of an infinite good, which is Heaven, and the incurring of an infinite evil, which is Hell; and both for eternity. Here pause awhile and raise your eyes to Heaven. Behold Jesus sitting at the right hand of His Heavenly Father, next to Him a multitude of elect in inexpressible glory and bliss. Who are those, pray tell me, who are nearest to Jesus? Oh! Be astonished; the Apostles, who as impostors were driven from city to city, were cast into chains, were everywhere persecuted and con emned to death; monks and hermits and apostolic men, who labored for the honor of God, amid thousands of insults and contumelies; holy virgins, who suffered with patience and in silence so many affronts, railleries, and trying vexations. As they were on earth close to Jesus in suffering, so they are now high in Heaven and close to Him in glory. Next, turn your eyes down to the infernal depths; behold there Satan tormented in an ocean of fire and brimstone, and around him a multitude of reprobates in excruciating pains and tortures. But who are those who are down so low in hell and so near to Satan? Ah! the mighty lords and grand ladies who were worshipped and adored on earth. These lords and ladies were in the highest positions, honors, dignities. Their foolish pride has brought them to these pains. These men and women who could refuse nothing to the desires of the flesh are plunged by their carnal pleasures into this misery. On earth they listened to the insidious invitations of Satan, and are now with him deep, very deep in Hell.

AFFECTIONS.

The more I contemplate Thee, O Jesus, the clearer I see that neither in my understanding has there been any knowledge of truth, nor in my will any love of virtue. On earth Thou didst esteem nothing but poverty and privations, pains and hardships. These things Thou didst regard as the surest means to sanctity and to a high degree of glory in Heaven. Thou didst despise riches and temporal blessings, the honor and applause of men, the delights of the senses, and didst look on them as the most dangerous allurements for the unwary to beguile them into Hell. O what reason have not I to feel shame and confusion! I dare not lift up my eyes to Thee on the Cross. What Thou didst esteem, I despise; what Thou didst seek, I flee; what Thou didst love, I hate. The invitations which the Devil makes please us; the inspirations which Thou, O my Jesus, givest, displease me. It is just as if I had tacitly made a resolution to follow Satan, and not to follow Thee. What then shall I do? I must follow Thee, O Jesus! Henceforth I must regard Thee as the only leader to sanctity and perfection.

POINT III.

Whom We are to follow—Jesus or Satan—may be seen by the End for which God has called Us to the Religious State.

Bring to mind once more your last end. You were, under God's guidance, cheered on to religious life, that you might honor and love God here more perfectly than seculars, and eternally possess Him hereafter in a higher glory. But to honor and love Him thus, you must closely follow Jesus Christ. Examine thoroughly the truth I now present to your consideration:

1st. The calling to perfection is an extraordinary grace. God is infinite power, infinite wisdom, and the inexhaustible source of every good. And yet, notwithstanding all these perfections, He can give nothing greater and more excellent than perfect love and union with Him. This is the grace of all graces, the summary of all the mercies of God, and the most precious jewel of all His riches. According to the testimony of St. John Chrysostom, a soul that arrives at perfection is in the sight of God better than ten thousand ordinary Christians.

2d. One can attain to perfection only by the means which God has appointed. To raise a soul to perfection is an act of the greatest mercy of God. He is as little obliged to bestow this grace on you as a mighty king to make a poor country girl a queen, and to place her next to himself on the throne. Whatever conditions God, according to His Divine pleasure, imposes for attaining this inestimable grace, you must fulfil, and whatever means He prescribes you must employ.

3d. These means are the universal and perfect imitation of Jesus Christ. "I am the door"—these are the very words of our dear Lord—"by Me, if any man enter in, he shall be saved; and he shall go in, and go out, and shall find pastures" (St. John x. 9). "This is My beloved Son," says the Heavenly Father, "in whom I have pleased Myself; hear ye Him" (2 Pet. i. 17). The door to sanctity then is Jesus. The model of holiness is Jesus. If you enter by this door you will acquire perfection, the purest love of God, and the most intimate union with Him.

AFFECTIONS.

Faith.—How far above the understanding of men are Thy judgments, O God! Thou art the eternal truth; I have but to assent. I believe that true riches consist in poverty, true glory in contempt, true peace in the testimony of a good conscience, true liberty in subjection, and the true way to holiness in following Thee. Any other way is nothing else but the caricature of virtue, but deception, but hypocrisy, all which cannot stand in Thy sight.

Desire of Union with God.—Thou art, O Lord, my only and supreme good, in whom all my happiness is centred. I sigh after Thee with all the powers of my soul. I must love Thee in this world and love Thee perfectly, that I may enjoy Thee in the glory which Thou hast prepared from eternity for those who follow Thee. This ineffable consolation here on earth and hereafter must be purchased by continued self-abnegation and heroic virtue. Nature may repine; still I am fully determined to follow Thee, O Jesus. And how can I refuse? Can it be too hard to love, on account of Thee, ill-disposed and perverse persons, since for my sake Thou didst pray on the Cross for Thy executioners? Why should not I, a guilty creature, suffer a little for Thee, since Thou hast suffered so much for me?

O give me Thy spirit, Thy obedient spirit, Thy humble spirit, Thy meek spirit, and Thy charitable spirit, and I will bless Thee and glorify Thee on earth, so as to be able to bless and glorify Thee in Heaven.

Intermediate Meditation 2.
THE THREE CLASSES OF MEN.

POINT I.

TO THE FIRST CLASS BELONG THOSE WHO AIM AT PERFECTION, BUT ONLY IN DESIRE; THEY SPEAK OF IT CONTINUALLY, BUT DO NOT WISH IT SINCERELY.

Let us visit in spirit an hospital of ordinary patients. Here lies one with a burning fever. It speedily increases and death is feared. The physician is called, and declares the sickness fatal but not irremediable, provided the medicine which he prescribes be faithfully taken. This is the very thing which displeases the sick person, who keeps repeating, "I desire with all my heart to be restored to health, but I wish none of your medicines. These I cannot and will not take." Does this patient really wish to be cured? From the hospital let us go to the cell of a religious, who has been in a fearful state of long-standing tepidity. The evil, however, may be remedied by a firm resolve and a determined will, by saying all prayers with fervor, by performing all works in the spirit of love and a pure intention, by walking in the presence of God, by frequent aspirations, and by courageous self-denial. This does not at all please a tepid religious, who continually says, "I wish with all my heart to attain to perfection, but these means I cannot and I will not use." Has this religious an earnest desire to arrive at perfection?

Let us now consider the evils of tepidity.

(1.) Such tepidity is why God allows the soul to fall into grievous sins.

He manifests this by two comparisons. The first He takes from a field: "The earth that drinketh in the rain which cometh upon it, and bringeth forth thorns and briers, is reprobate and very near unto a curse" (Heb. vi. 7, 8).

The second He takes from lukewarm water, which nobody can long bear without loathing and disgust. "Because thou art lukewarm, and neither cold nor hot, I will begin to vomit thee out of My mouth" (Apoc. iii. 16).

(2.) Such tepidity is why God finally allows the soul to perish.

This truth He again explains in two comparisons: The first is drawn from a tree on the wayside, which He curses: "Seeing a certain fig-tree, He came to it and found nothing on it but leaves only, and He saith to it, May no fruit grow on thee henceforth forever. And immediately the fig-tree withered away" (St. Matt. xxi. 19). The second is taken from a tree in a garden. The owner of a garden found a tree for three successive years without fruit. He turned to the gardener and said to him, "Behold for these three years I come, seeking fruit on this fig-tree, and I find none. Cut it down therefore; why cumbereth it the ground?" (St. Luke xiii. 7).

AFFECTIONS.

Fear.—I am struck with terror when I consider these words which Thou hast spoken; I may be lost yet, I whom Thou hast called to a religious life in preference to so many thousands, I on whom Thou hast showered such a multitude of graces. O cursed tepidity! thou must indeed be a great evil, since thou may be the cause of my being cast off forever by a God of infinite mercy.

Compunction.—Have patience with me a while, O Jesus! I detest and bewail from my inmost soul all the negligences of which I have been guilty. I am sorry for the abuse of so many of Thy graces and mercies. Until now I have lived in such a manner that I have neither taken a serious care of Thy honor nor of the salvation of my immortal soul. Through Thy mercy, O Jesus, I now see my wickedness, and I am resolved for the future to follow Thee closely.

POINT II.

TO THE SECOND CLASS BELONG THOSE WHO WISH, IT IS TRUE, TO AIM AT PERFECTION, BUT HAVE NOT A UNIVERSAL AND GENEROUS WILL.

Let us return once more to the sick-room. Lo! here lies another person entirely different from the first. This person desires to be restored to health, and for this purpose is ready to employ the means, but not all; objects to burning and cutting and other painful methods. What are we to say of this patient? There is a will, but not a strong, universal and heroic will. In the same condition are many religious. They desire to arrive at perfection, and in order to obtain it they are ready to employ the means, but not all. Interior dereliction and darkness, aridity and grievous, long-lasting temptations, unmerited humiliations and contempt, and other trials and tribulations of the same sort are too trying for them. But what will be the consequences of this half will? Consider them, and let them sink deeply into your mind.

(1.) Such a soul leads a life without consolation. If we do not give ourselves to God without reserve, our bad inclinations and inordinate affections never die. Pride and love of honor, stubbornness and obstinacy, the unrestrained use of the tongue, sadness and uncharitable conversation are as strong and as vigorous after twenty years as at the first entrance into religion.

They even increase with time, like a sapling which grows every year higher and broader. Such a one will feel more and more the yoke of obedience, bear contempt more and more unwillingly, in words become freer, and in the intercourse with others more and more irritable. An unmortified passion in the soul is the same as a viper in the bosom. How long can one remain without wounds and pains? As long as the viper remains quiet. As soon as it awakens from its dormant state it gnaws and torments. Likewise how long is a tepid soul without trouble? As long as its evil affections are at rest. If contempt or an injury be inflicted, or a harsh and unpleasing command given, it fires up and vents its anger on all around. How blind we are! We see not the source of our misery. We seek the evil everywhere, but not in our soul where it certainly is.

(2.) Such a soul leads a life without making any progress in perfection. God has pronounced the sentence which shall never be changed: "Every one of you that doth not renounce all that he possesseth cannot be My disciple" (St. Luke xiv. 33). That is to say, they who die not entirely to creatures, and give themselves up without reserve to My guidance, cannot arrive at My love and at union with Me. Why so? Hear the reason.

1st. God is Supreme Master. He is free to give or not to whom He pleases the special graces which are necessary for perfection. Now

He has decreed that He will not give them to any soul except it gives itself up to Him without reserve. Who dares to call in question this mode of acting?

2d. God is a supreme excellence. It is His due that we consecrate to Him our whole heart, with all its affections. He will never forego this right, nor ever admit a soul to union with Him that reserves to itself the least trifle.

AFFECTIONS.

Acknowledgment.—This sick person who has the will to regain health, provided it be without any painful operation, or without bitter medicine, is a true image of my soul. I desire perfect humility without humiliation and contempt; perfect obedience without any severe test; perfect charity and meekness without suffering any injury. How foolishly have I acted! Without suffering patiently and joyfully no one before me became a saint. I must suffer, I must die to myself, if I wish to arrive at perfection. I will, then, suffer with Thee, and I will suffer till all evil affections have died out.

Resolution.—Shall I hate myself so much as to choose rather the greater cross and fly from the smaller? A little pride causes in the heart more trouble and confusion than the most profound humility; a little anger stirs up the soul more than the greatest meekness; a little stubbornness torments the mind more than the most perfect obedience. If suffering must necessarily be my portion, either for virtue or for vice, I prefer to suffer for virtue. In this case I shall suffer for Heaven, and for Thee, O Jesus!

POINT III.

To the Third Class belong Those who have an Earnest and Generous Wish to arrive at Perfection, and are ready to do what God demands, and to suffer all that He requires for Holiness of Life.

These are the advantages of this class:

(1.) A soul thus impressed will surely arrive at perfection.

The more we give ourselves up to God, the more He communicates Himself to us. To a soul, therefore, that gives itself entirely up to Him, He gives Himself without reserve.

(2.) A soul acting thus shall certainly acquire close union with God.

Union and intimate familiarity with God is the reward promised to perfect love. "If any one love Me," says our Divine Redeemer, "he will keep My word, and My Father will love him, and We will come to him and will make Our abode with him" (St. John, xiv. 23).

(3.) A soul, surrendering itself without reserve, infallibly obtains from Him graces of the highest order.

God is infinite liberality; He pours plenteously His graces into a soul that consecrates itself entirely to Him. These are, the sweetest tranquillity, peace, joy of heart, and the most tender affection for Him. This is the hundred-fold which Christ has promised to those who for His love have quitted all and even themselves.

AFFECTIONS.

Fear.—O my God, how mercifully Thou dealest with me! Through Thy grace I now know the way which leads to sanctity. I see that *I* shall infallibly arrive at it, if I only give myself up to Thee. But "unto whomsoever much is given"—these are Thy words—"of him much shall be required; and to whom they have committed much, of him they will demand the more" (St. Luke xii. 48). Oh, what a misfortune would it be for me if the abundance of graces which should raise me higher in Heaven would only plunge me deeper in Hell! There are many souls that have no medium; they either ascend very high in Heaven or descend very low into Hell.

Resolution.—I will then in time be on my guard, and walk in the way which Thy Divine light has shown me to-day. This moment I give myself wholly to Thy guidance. The only thing I ask is this: Give me the grace that I may love Thee, all the rest I leave to Thy most holy will. Whatever adversities and trials occur, I will regard them as the ordinances of Thy fatherly providence, and use them with the most perfect submission as means to sanctity.

SIXTH DAY.

Intermediate Meditation 3.

ON THE THIRD DEGREE OF HUMILITY, OR THE LOVE OF CONTEMPT.

POINT I.

IT IS JUST THAT WE LOVE CONTEMPT.

So blind are we and self-esteem is so deeply rooted in our hearts, that we believe that the greatest injustice is done to us when we are despised, and yet it is certain that nothing but contempt is our due, and that all men on earth are not able to despise us as much as we deserve. In the sight of God, who is truth itself, the high notions we entertain of our own merit are nothing but error and falsehood; the desire we have to be esteemed, praised and honored is nothing but injustice; and that vainglory, that height we aspire after, is in fact the depth of degradation. I will now fully unfold this truth to you.

1st. God must punish sin. Faith teaches it. God is infinite goodness, and must reward the good; He is infinite justice, and must punish the wicked.

2d. God can punish sin as He pleases. God has infinite dominion. He can punish sin by pains both for the body and for the soul. The most suitable is contempt, for as sin is the contemning of God, it is just that it be punished by contempt. Can there be anything more equitable than that the sinner, who has dared to despise an infinitely great God, should be likewise despised in return?

3d. God can punish sin through whom He pleases. He punished David's through his own son; the disobedient prophet's by a lion which tore him into pieces (3 Kings xiii. 26); Heliodorus's by two angels who scourged him, without ceasing, with many stripes (2 Mach. iii. 26); and in His only begotten Son, Jesus Christ, He punished our sins by a traitorous Apostle and by brutal executioners. He can also punish you through whom He pleases.

4th. How much soever God may punish sin He always punishes it less than it deserves. Should you live to the end of the world and be continually abused, calumniated and persecuted, you could not therewith repair the contempt which one venial sin throws on the Divine Majesty. Have you committed no sins? Would to Heaven it were so; but alas! you have been guilty of hundreds, perhaps of thousands. How many and how great soever the humiliations He may send you, they will always be fewer and less than you have deserved. Hence it follows that you cannot complain of contempt on the part of any one. In all trials, therefore, you should praise God, because it is just that contempt be ever your lot.

AFFECTIONS.

An Act of Self-abasement.—It is right, O my God, I acknowledge it, yes, it is right that I be contemned. What are all the insults of this earth in comparison with those I have deserved? If I have ever defiled myself by a single mortal sin, I should be in Hell! I should then deserve to be forever cursed by all the elect of Heaven, and insulted by all the damned in Hell. Thou hast spared me, O my God, this shame, and instead of eternal curses and maledictions, Thou art satisfied that I suffer contempt on earth. Should I not then regard it as an effect of Thy mercy and bear it cheerfully?

Resolution.—May this thought never be effaced from my memory: I have sinned and deserved that Heaven and Hell, angels and men, the elect and the reprobate, should abuse me eternally.

POINT II.

OUR OWN INTEREST REQUIRES THAT WE LOVE CONTEMPT.

In contempt, nothing can be found but what is bitter and displeasing; but many things of this sort we like even when they are distasteful by their nature, if only they are beneficial. Nothing more agreeable can be brought to a sick person than a bitter medicine, provided it reanimates and cures. Why, then, should we not love contempt, since it brings us so great and desirable advantages?

First advantage.—Contempt destroys pride. The greatest impediments to perfection are pride and vanity. As long as the least self-esteem and self-complacency, or the slightest love of honor, reigns in your soul, so long God does not take up His abode therein. He holds it in detestation, and leaves it devoid of heavenly light, of holy affections, without special graces and without the special guidance of His Divine providence. What is the remedy for this evil of pride? The surest, the most certain and the quickest remedy is contempt. There is nothing better to extinguish fire than a heavy rain, and to destroy pride nothing is more efficacious than contempt. Without this remedy few souls reach true humility. Should you not, therefore, ardently desire contempt? Should you not, whenever you meet with it, bear it joyfully, and praise and bless God for allowing it to fall on you? We thank a physician who, though we suffer much, successfully performs an operation on us; why should we not thank God who, even through harsh means, frees us from our accursed pride?

Second advantage.—Contempt implants humility. The best preparation for union with God is humility. When God sees it in a soul He takes immediate possession of it and showers on it His choicest graces. An humble soul is like a valley; for, as all mountain waters flow into the valley during rainy weather, so also heavenly graces flee the proud, and are gathered in the depth of an humble soul.

What are the means to acquire this virtue so pleasing to God? Look at Jesus and learn from Him to love contempt. Our beloved Redeemer has shown us in every virtue the fittest means for its attainment, and for humility there is nothing else but contempt and persecution, and perpetual silence in suffering them.

AFFECTIONS.

O Jesus, my Redeemer, my All! I now see well what displeases Thee in my heart, and what prevents Thee from dwelling therein. The seeking of the esteem and the applause of others is the evil which renders my heart so hateful to Thee. As long as I do not root out this inclination I cannot come to Thee, O Saviour! A God who loves humility, and a soul that loves pride, cannot be familiarly united. This detestable love of honor is so deeply engrafted in my soul that it seems it cannot be completely uprooted. I have resolved over and over to put it down, and, nevertheless, I still discern it in my heart. My resolutions were only empty words. Had I been in earnest, I would have sincerely loved those who despised me; had I been in earnest, I would have been well pleased with every humiliation that came upon me. O merciful Jesus, destroy in me all love of honor, in order that Thou alone mayest reign in my heart.

POINT III.

Its Very Excellence requires that We Love Contempt.

Did we but know how precious before God the loving of contempt is, we would willingly and joyfully undergo the hardships for which our nature feels a repugnance. Let us then consider the excellence of bearing contempt silently.

First excellence.—It is the greatest sacrifice you can make in this life. We think only of exalting and advancing ourselves. Our own superiority is the point to which all our thoughts and desires of the mind centre. Persons who forego all pleasures, and chastise their bodies by fasting, watching and other austerities, love solitude and spend many hours every day in prayer, who patiently endure excruciating pains of the body, are sometimes unable to bear silently calumny, contempt, or even a harsh rebuke. This suffices to shipwreck their whole sanctity. For pride cannot be extirpated without a complete victory over nature. This, therefore, is the greatest sacrifice which we can offer to God.

Second excellence.—To suffer contempt silently is the characteristic mark of the following of Christ.

Our Lord met contempt at every step. He did not always preach, did not always pray, did not always suffer, was not always sad; but always was contemned. Thus, He was at His birth in a stable, as a child in His flight into Egypt, as a youth in the workshop of Nazareth, in His mature age when He appeared publicly, and at His death on the Cross. His doctrine, His virtues and His miracles were despised. He was despised in His humanity and His divinity. No one, therefore, can have the love of Jesus Christ without the love of contempt.

Third excellence.—To suffer contempt silently is the key to the Heart of Jesus and the opening to union with Him. In vain do we seek Jesus Christ without contempt. Neither prayer, nor fasting, nor watching, nor any other exercise suffices except dying to self and dying by contempt. This alone is the spirit of Jesus Christ.

Jesus loves souls that thus die and no others; these He enlightens, and to them He reveals His secrets. He sweetens their troubles and makes them find their delight in crosses. With these He keeps up familiar intercourse and admits them to union with Himself. To them these words of Holy Writ apply: "Behold! I stand at the gate and knock; if any man shall hear My voice and open to Me the door, I will come in to him and will sup with him and he with Me" (Apoc. iii. 20). Are we not then foolish and inconsiderate in being troubled by contempt? Should we not ardently desire a good, which Jesus prizes so highly?

AFFECTIONS.

The love of honor must, therefore, die in my soul, and that of contempt must live therein continually; otherwise I can never be interiorly purified. Accept then, O God, the oblation which I now make.

(1.) I detest and put away forever all love of honor; I do not wish any one to be occupied for a single instant with me in thought, or esteem, or love; supposing this should happen against my will, I forego the pleasure which may spring therefrom as something which is an abomination in Thy sight.

(2.) I love and choose with all my heart the state of contempt. Whatever may befall me in it, through Thy mercy, I will for Thy sake bear silently, and praise and bless Thee.

(3.) In Thy hands I place now whatever right I may have to my honor and reputation. I will care for it no more than if it were another's good. Accept, O Jesus, this sacrifice; I will renew it every day and in it I desire to live and die.

PRAYER TO OBTAIN THE SPIRIT OF HUMILITY.

Without Thee, O Jesus, all my good desires will vanish like smoke; without Thee I shall never carry out my resolutions. Look, then, on me, O dearest Jesus, with an eye of pity. Give me a heart like unto Thine! Grant that I may love all Thou hast loved, and detest whatever Thou hast detested.

Meditation 1.

On the Mental Sufferings of Christ in the Garden of Gethsemane.

POINT I.

CHRIST HAS LED THE WAY IN SUFFERING ALL THE MENTAL TRIALS WHICH ARE MET WITH ON THE ROAD TO PERFECTION.

The adorable Heart of our dear Redeemer suffered the most terrible anguish and distress. Remember, however, that the Divinity gave Christ as little assistance as the soul of one of the elect gives its mouldering body. He has suffered as He would have suffered had He been a mere man like yourself. His first suffering was overwhelming sadness. Its causes were two-fold: The first was his ardent love for us No mother ever loved her only child as tenderly as Jesus Christ loved each one of us. The second was His Omniscience. He foreknew that, notwithstanding His passion and death, the greater number of wretched mortals would be eternally lost. Thence arose sadness so intense that it alone would have sufficed to deprive Him of life. Great was the sorrow of the heartbroken mothers whose babes were butchered by Herod's cruel order. Greater still that of Jesus on foreseeing the countless millions that would be lost forever.

The second suffering of Christ was fear. The expectation of death is a terrible torture. It has happened more than once that when death was announced to the young and healthy, their hair became grey in one night through terror. The soul of Jesus suffered far more from the fear of His own death, because there never has been one who could represent to himself, as Jesus could, the impending death with its bitter accompaniments.

The third suffering of Christ was an inward struggle. This struggle was between His human and Divine nature. The former felt extreme reluctance to suffer and die in this way, and forced Him to cry out, "Father, if it be possible, let this chalice pass away." It, however, overcame this repugnance and revoked the first petition, in these words, "Not My will but Thine be done." This struggle was so fearful that a bloody sweat trickled down from His body and ensanguined the ground on which He lay prostrate.

The fourth suffering of Christ was the agony of death. Nothing more terrible can befall us than the agony of death. A cold sweat bedews our foreheads; our hands and feet become stiff and torpid; we breathe by gasps, till our last convulsive shudder. Let us look now at Jesus in His agony. Instead of sweat, drops of blood run down; He falls on the ground; His heart throbs violently; He suffers, as it were, the agony of death. He would have died thereof, had not an angel comforted and strengthened Him, in order that He might consummate on the Cross the sacrifice for the redemption of the world.

AFFECTIONS.

Astonishment.—O Jesus, Thou wast plunged in a sea of bitterness, of horror, of torment, of agony and of desolation! In this horrible condition I behold in Thee the greatest constancy. Thou didst lift up Thy hands towards Heaven and pray; Thou didst submit to the will of Thy Heavenly Father and prepare Thyself for Thy death on the Cross. This is to love truly and to seek nothing but the Divine pleasure. What are my sufferings compared with Thine, most afflicted Jesus? And, nevertheless, how soon they overpower me! I am poured out on exterior things and I am seldom recollected. I feel diffident of Thy mercy. These are the unhappy fruits that dereliction produces in my soul. I am filled with confusion before Thee. Thou art innocence itself and art overwhelmed with sadness. I am a sinner and desire naught but consolation.

Resolution.—Jesus without a single sin is sorrowful unto death, and I, after so many sins, desire to be consoled until death. Henceforth it shall be enough for me to please my blessed Redeemer. Him alone will I seek. Him alone will I love, in darkness or in light, in dereliction or in consolation.

POINT II.

THE STATE OF DERELICTION IS MORE PROFITABLE TO US THAN THAT OF CONSOLATION.

What peace of mind would we not enjoy in the midst of darkness and dereliction by remembering how profitable this state may be to our dearest interests! To have an idea of it, let us consider the following truths:

First Truth.—The state of dereliction is more agreeable to God than that of consolation. When our minds are at peace, and devotion swells our hearts, we are satisfied. How blind we are! A day of dereliction is incomparably better than one of consolation, for, on this latter day, God gives us something, but we give nothing to God. He invites us to His table and allows us to taste His sweetness. There is liberality on the part of God towards us, and none on our part towards Him. In consolation God can find many souls that are faithful, but few that are in dereliction. To be deprived of all light and consolation, and nevertheless to persevere fervently in prayer, and to be constant in interior recollection, in mortification, and in other exercises, while we are assailed and tormented with temptations, is a sacrifice most pleasing to God.

Second Truth.—The state of dereliction brings the soul more safely and quickly to the perfect love of God and union with Him than the state of consolation. To love God perfectly consists in seeking in all things only His Divine will. But what can lead us more securely thither than the state of dereliction? For a soul that is faithful in this state deprives herself of all earthly consolation, and God deprives her of all interior consolation. Thus it becomes, as it were, crucified and dead to self and all creatures. When the window-curtain is raised in a room the sun pours into it rays of light and warmth. So it is with the soul; as soon as it divests itself of all attachments to creatures, God sends into it the rays of His light and the heat of His love. How desirable then is the state of desolation! As fire purifies gold, and consumes all dross, so the state of dereliction purifies the soul, and destroys in it every inclination to sin.

AFFECTIONS.

Oblation.—I behold Jesus in a state of dereliction, and sorrowful unto death. I also see that the state of dereliction is extremely profitable to me, for it brings me to union with Him. Now, then, I offer myself wholly to Thee. O Lord! I am ready to be deprived of all comfort, whether it be from Heaven or earth, of all light and of all consolation. I am ready to suffer interiorly and exteriorly, and to bear with darkness of mind abandonment and temptations as Thou willest. My only consolation, henceforth, shall be the accomplishment of Thy most holy will.

A Prayer to Obtain Fortitude.—I raise my heart and hands to Thee, O Jesus, to implore Thy mercy. To be deprived of all heavenly consolations, and to seek none on this earth; to feel only darkness in my understanding, only dryness in my will and troubles in my heart, and, nevertheless, to persevere fervently in prayer; to be assailed by temptations, and yet to lead a life of recollection and walk in Thy presence; to feel nothing but bitterness and universal uprising of disorderly affections, and still to be meek, gentle and charitable towards my neighbor, is something very arduous. For so great an undertaking special graces are needed, and for these graces I turn to Thee, O dearest Lord!

NOTE.—In place of the Third Meditation of the day, one of the preceding Meditations is to be repeated.

SEVENTH DAY.

Meditation 2.

ON THE BODILY SUFFERINGS OF JESUS CHRIST WHILE HANGING ON THE CROSS.

POINT I.

WE CAN NEVER SUFFER IN OUR BODIES WHAT JESUS HAS SUFFERED IN HIS BODY.

To understand something of the greatness of the pains which Christ felt we merely have to consider the circumstances.

First circumstance.—The pains of Christ were in every part and in every member of the body. Look in imagination at His whole body. The hair and beard torn out; His countenance disfigured; His eyes blood-shot; His cheeks swollen with blows; His mouth shrivelled; His head everywhere pierced with thorns; His hands and feet bored through with nails, and His flesh bruised and mangled all over. His whole body was but one continued wound! Isaias speaks thus of the suffering of Jesus, "He hath borne our infirmities and carried our sorrows, and we have thought Him, as it were, a leper, and as one struck by God and afflicted" (Isaias liii. 4).

Second circumstance.—The pains of Jesus were unspeakably cruel and incomparably greater than those ever suffered by any man. Why so? First on account of the delicacy of His frame and the tenderness of His flesh. "The body of our Lord," says St. Bonaventure, "was more sensitive on the sole of His feet than others are in the pupil of the eye." Secondly.—The most sensitive parts of the body were most cruelly tortured. The thorns were so deeply forced into the head that they penetrated and pierced through the flesh and nerves. The nails were driven by violent strokes of the hammer through hands and feet. Fearfully excruciating must have been the torment, as the whole weight of the body hung for three long hours from these nails.

Third circumstance.—The pains of Jesus were without any, even the least, alleviation. He had been hanging on the Cross for two hours; all but a few drops of His blood was shed; His thirst was so burning that He cried out for relief by saying, "I thirst," and yet He was offered but vinegar and gall to increase His torment.

AFFECTIONS.

Thanksgiving.—I know not, O Jesus, what to think or say of this terrible scene. All this Thou hast suffered on account of my sins. Faith teaches this. Thy bloody sweat, being treated as a fool, Thy scourging and crowning with thorns, and Thy death on the Cross, all Thy sufferings, O Jesus, were for my sins. All possible thanks, my Saviour, for every drop of blood which Thou hast shed for me; for all the ignominy, outrages and insults which Thou hast suffered for my sake; for all the pains and torments which Thou hast endured on the Cross.

Resolution.—But mere thanks are not sufficient. I must make Thee, O Jesus, a return for Thy love. Here is now my irrevocable offering: Thou foreknowest the pains, the troubles, and the infirmities of the body that are preordained for me. From this out I submit to all these preordinances, and beseech Thee to carry them out fully in my regard. Thou foreseest, O Jesus, when and by what death I am to leave this world; this appointment I humbly revere and accept. Order the way, the manner, the place of my death. One thing only I ask, and that daily, to die the death of the just. I will suffer and die through love of Thee, as Thou hast suffered and died through love for me.

POINT II.

Christ's Patience was as Wonderful as His Pains were Terrible.

These circumstances will illustrate it fully:

1st Circumstance. Jesus bore in silence all His pains. Holy Writ compares Christ to a meek lamb; for as it allows itself to be shorn or led to slaughter without resistance or cry, thus also Jesus allowed Himself to be tormented and led to death without a complaint. Jesus's whole body was fearfully mangled; He kept silence. Jesus was crowned with thorns; He kept silence. Jesus took the Cross on His shoulders and, though extremely weak, had to drag it along; still He kept silence. His hands and feet were dug with nails; He kept silence. "He was as a dumb man not opening His mouth," says the prophet (Ps. xxxvii. 14). Thus Jesus acted under the most violent pains, and what do I do?

2d Circumstance. Jesus suffered the pains with meekness. There never has been one who had better reasons to feel indignant than Jesus on the Cross. He was hated by all. The hearts of all who stood around were known to Him. He saw in them only hatred and ill-will, and that they were delighted with His pains. He was mocked and insulted by the Pharisees and Scribes. "Vah!" said they, "Thou that destroyest the temple of God, and in three days dost rebuild it, save Thy own self; if Thou be the Son of God come down from the Cross. He saved others, Himself He cannot save. If He be the king of Israel, let Him now come down from the Cross, and we will believe Him" (St. Matt. xxvii. 40–42). He suffers all with the most perfect resignation and with the most ardent love, so that He felt more keenly the perdition of His enemies than His own pains, for He said to the women, "Daughters of Jerusalem, weep not over Me, but weep for yourselves and for your children" (St. Luke xxiii. 28).

3d Circumstance. Jesus suffered the pains with fortitude, and with the desire of suffering more. Jesus hangs on the Cross, His whole strength is exhausted, His pains have increased to the highest degree. Look into His heart and admire its fortitude. A two-fold love and a two-fold desire burn in it. He loved His Heavenly Father, and desired to have more strength to suffer still more for Him. He also loved us with an infinite love, and therefore desired to live longer and to suffer still more for us.

AFFECTIONS.

Self-Confusion.—What confusion comes over me when I behold Thee, O Jesus, hanging on the Cross! How hast Thou sinned, O revered head of my Redeemer, that Thou art pierced with so many sharp thorns? How have you sinned, O beautiful eyes of my Saviour, that you are so clotted with blood? What have you done omnipotent hands and feet, that you are so cruelly perforated with nails? What hast Thou done, O most loving Heart, that Thou art pierced by the lance? My sins lacerated Jesus's body, my sins nailed Him to the Cross, my sins caused His death.

Acknowledgment and Resolution.—After my sins have done this I will suffer nothing, I will not even acknowledge that I have deserved to suffer; but, by the light of Thy grace, I come to know it now. There is no pain on earth which I have not deserved; there is no torment in Hell which I have not merited. All I have suffered, till now, is not enough to satisfy for one sin. How unjust then are my murmurs and complaints! I always suffer less than I have deserved. Henceforth I submit wholly to Thy will, and I adore Thy appointments in the midst of my sufferings.

Meditation 3.

ON THE AFFRONTS AND OUTRAGES WHICH JESUS SUFFERED.

POINT I.

THERE NEVER HAS BEEN ONE AND NEVER WILL THERE BE ONE WHO SUFFERED SUCH AFFRONTS AND OUTRAGES AS JESUS CHRIST.

It is impossible to enumerate them all. Consider some of them, and they will suffice to fill you with confusion and to extinguish your pride.

1st. False accusations. Without doubt nothing is harder for a noble soul to bear than crimes falsely imputed. Let us enter the courts of Annas and Caiphas and hear the crimes attributed to Jesus. The witnesses are there, and what do they say? O unheard-of blasphemy! They say, He takes His repasts with notorious sinners. He is a man of intolerable pride and declares Himself to be God. He spreads impious doctrines and misleads the people. He works miracles by the help of Satan, and as a sorcerer He has secret dealings. Thus the false witnesses spoke of Jesus in the courts of the high-priests, thus they shouted before Pilate's tribunal, thus they cried out in the streets of Jerusalem.

2d. The ridicule and mockery.—These impious men were not satisfied with accusing Jesus as a blasphemer, they also make Him out a fool. He stands before Herod's tribunal. He keeps silence. Therefore He must suffer affront. "You think too much of this man," said Herod. "He is a fool." At these words of the angry king Jesus was clothed in a fool's garment, and in this apparel He was led through the city amidst the insults and blasphemies of a mocking rabble. This was not the only affront, another followed in Pilate's court. The soldiers, instigated by the Jews who were in the crowd, made sport of our Lord, heaping upon Him indignities which Hell alone could suggest: they threw a tattered purple garment on His shoulders, they put a reed in His hand as sceptre, they pressed a crown of thorns on His head, they gave Him blows on the cheeks, they spat in His face, they bent their knees in derision before Him. Heaven was astonished at these insults, and the angelic choirs wept. The multitude joyfully looked on and by their sneers, laughter and joyful shouts, increased the pains of Jesus.

3d. The iniquitous sentence of death.—Pilate

led Jesus, whose innocence he well knew, before the people, and at the same time he also brought out Barabbas, and said, "Whom will you that I release to you, Barabbas or Jesus, that is called Christ?" Pilate believed that Jesus would be preferred; they however cried out with one voice, "Away with this man, release unto us Barabbas." Who was Barrabas? A seditious man and a murderer; for the Holy Scriptures tell us "that he was for a certain sedition and for a murder cast into prison." Then Pilate "released to them Barabbas, and delivered Jesus unto them to be crucified." This death was the most ignominious and the most infamous; He was crucified between two robbers as if He was the most wicked. Jesus drags up the Cross to Calvary amid the scornful shouts and clamors of the high-priests, and the blasphemous derisions of the Pharisees and Scribes, amid the scoffing laughter and mockery of an innumerable people, to fulfil the words of the prophet, " I am a worm and no man: the reproach of men and the outcast of the people" (Ps. xxi. 7).

Pause here and reflect. 1st. Did God the Father act unjustly in ordaining these outrages for His only begotten Son? No! Jesus took upon Himself our sins, and for these sins deserved all He suffered. 2d. Would God treat you injustly in appointing for you affronts and insults like unto those of His only begotten Son? No! Sin deserves it, and your conscience tells you that you have sinned. If you believe that sins deserve

The Affronts and Outrages Jesus Suffered.

such affronts and insults, what intolerable pride then is it not on your part to refuse to suffer through love for Jesus, since He, for the love of you, suffered outrages so cruel?

AFFECTIONS.

Admiration of Jesus's Meekness.—O Jesus, dear Redeemer, how wonderful is Thy meekness and Thy humility! Thou art the infinite wisdom which governs Heaven and earth, and Thou didst pass as a fool. Thou wast ridiculed as a mock-king. Thou art infinite sanctity from which all heavenly graces flow, and Thou wast deemed a hypocrite, a Samaritan and a sorcerer. How didst thou suffer these insults? Meekly, humbly and silently. Thou didst submit to all of them with the most perfect resignation and without the least resistance. I will also henceforward suffer and endure in silence.

Self-confusion.—How detestable in Thy sight my pride must be! I, one whose understanding is so blind, wish to be thought wise, while Jesus was clad in the garment of a fool and dragged through the streets amidst blasphemous shouts. I, whose heart is full of disorders, wish to be honored, while Jesus was accused of being a seducer and a blasphemer. I, who have not a particle of solid virtue, desire to be loved by all and to be preferred to others, while Jesus was thought less than a murderer. How hateful must this my pride be to Thee, O Jesus! Have mercy on me and put into my mind other thoughts and into my will other affections.

POINT II.

THERE NEVER HAS BEEN ONE, AND NEVER WILL THERE BE ONE, WHO SUFFERED OUTRAGES AND INSULTS IN THE MANNER IN WHICH CHRIST SUFFERED THEM.

Speaking of this the royal prophet says, "He as a deaf man heard not, and was as a dumb man not opening His mouth" (Ps. xxxvii. 14). These words show us the depth of Christ's humility, and we may well be filled with wonder at His abasement.

1st. Christ was innocent. A thought never arose in His mind, a word never came to His lips, no act appeared in His life which was in any way blamable. The crimes which were imputed to Him were fabricated.

2d. Christ was omnipotent and infinitely wise. In an instant He could have crushed His enemies. Had He opened His lips His divine wisdom and eloquence would have put them to shame.

3d. Christ was omniscient. He knew how His enemies would misconstrue His silence, and that they would not cease to persecute Him till He was condemned to the most ignominious of deaths. He knew that those nearest and dearest to Him, His blessed mother and Apostles, would have to suffer for it. He saw that on account of it His miracles would be derided, His doctrine condemned, and His new Church most cruelly persecuted. All these reasons could not move Jesus to speak in His own defence. He kept silence, and He kept silence up to His last breath. What wonderful silence is this, O Jesus! What a profound lesson it inculcates! But, alas! how few are there who profit thereby! Where are the souls that, amidst contumely and affronts, keep silence with Jesus? They comply with everything else; they pray, they meditate, they mortify themselves; but to submit without complaint to unreasonable demands, to keep silence when ill treated, to love ignominy and humiliations, this is a burden which few shoulders can bear. Unless we follow Jesus, who is the only way to sanctity, we shall always remain little in His eyes, always contemptible, always hopeless of arriving at perfection.

AFFECTIONS.

Esteem and Love of Contempt.—How far above the wisdom of the world is Thy doctrine, O Jesus! In contempt and ignominy Thou seest all that is beautiful, all that is lovely. Hadst Thou spoken, Thou wouldst have had as much honor as Thou hadst insults; but Thou didst not long for honor but for outrages. I will then henceforth have the same thoughts as Thou hadst, love what Thou didst love, and regard contempt as a means of crushing my greatest enemy, pride, and of introducing Jesus into my heart.

Compunction and Resolution.—What sacrifice can there be more pleasing to Thy Divine

Majesty than that of sacrificing my honor and of bearing contempt in silence? The period of my life the richest in merit was not that in which I felt tender devotion towards God, but that when my best actions were criticised and blamed, and when I was most despised and insulted. I have then been deceived, O Jesus! I was troubled and became sad when I should have rejoiced; I fled from that which I should have sought; I murmured when I should have assented. Henceforth I will do as Thou didst do when the hour of Thy ignominy came. Thou didst then say, "that the world may know that I love the Father, arise, let us go hence" (St. John xiv. 31). This I will also say when contempt comes on me: that Heaven and earth may know that I love Jesus, let us arise and joyfully embrace contempt.

Meditation 4.

ON THE LOVE WHICH CHRIST ON THE CROSS HAS SHOWN FOR HIS ENEMIES.

POINT I.

THE LOVE OF JESUS WAS WONDERFUL ON ACCOUNT OF THE CIRCUMSTANCES AND OF THE HATRED AND RAGE OF HIS ENEMIES.

Jesus hangs on the Cross; His whole body is one wound; the pains are inconceivable. From

Him turn your eyes to those who surrounded Him in thousands, young and old, of every class and condition, Jews and Pagans, Pharisees and Scribes, the ancients of the people and high-priests. Few there were who took pity on Jesus; all hated and persecuted Him. Consider now the circumstances of this hatred and persecution.

The first was, the joy of His enemies. Jesus was not a mere man, but a Man-God, before whom all the hearts of those present lay open. He knew their thoughts; He read their malice; He saw their ill will while they shouted with joy at beholding Him on the Cross. They kept saying, This impostor deserved no better death; they rejoiced at His torments, and anxiously desired that His name might be forever blotted out. All this Jesus saw, and saw it in those for whose love He came down from Heaven, for whose sake He wrought so many miracles, for whose salvation He gave up His life on the Cross.

The second was the scorn and the derision of His enemies. We feel compassion for the most wicked man in his death-struggle, we even pity murderers on the scaffold, an universal silence reigns, sympathy shows itself on the countenance of the spectators. Quite otherwise was it with Jesus. The more excessive His pains and torments on the Cross, the more unrestrained was the scorn of His enemies. Vah! some said, Thou hast boasted to be able to destroy the temple of God, and in three days to build it up again; show now Thy power and save Thy own self. Vah! said others, He always trusted in God; let Him come now and deliver Him, if He will have Him, for He said, I am the Son of God. "Vah!" said the high-priests, "He saved others, Himself He cannot save. If He be the king of Israel, let Him now come down from the Cross, and we will believe Him" (Matt. xxvii. 39).

The third was the obstinacy of His enemies. Jesus bore His pains with infinite patience. He forgave His enemies and prayed for them to God, His Father, with wonderful meekness. All nature proclaimed His innocence and mourned. The sun was darkened, the earth trembled, the rocks split. All this the Jews saw, but did not cease to persecute Jesus. They blasphemed, mocked and cursed Him, and did so till His last breath. It would have been a great consolation for Him to foresee that, at least after His death, their hatred would discontinue; but no! He foreknew that they would laugh to scorn the miracles of the new law, that they would persecute the Apostles who announced the Gospel, that this stubbornness would last till their death, and that they would blaspheme Him in Hell forever. How hard, then, was it not, to love, these impious and accursed men? Behold on Mount Calvary the multitude of wicked priests who rejoiced that they had brought Jesus to an ignominious death, of wicked Pharisees who gathered together only for the purpose of insulting Him in His pains, of wicked executioners who nailed Him to the Cross. Has the world ever seen men more deserving of hatred than these? Now turn your eyes to the Cross, and see Jesus like an innocent lamb about to be slaughtered. Heaven admires His meekness. He prayed that the blood which He was shedding might bring salvation to His crucifiers. Consider now the persons whom you suppose it is hard to love. Are they false witnesses, who accuse you in the criminal courts? Are they inhuman beings, who have nothing to offer you in your weakness but vinegar and gall? Are they bloodthirsty mortals, who wish to nail you like Jesus on the Cross? No! They are persons whose countenances are sometimes unkind, and who sometimes speak roughly to you. It cannot be very hard to love these your enemies, since Jesus has loved His.

AFFECTIONS.

Self-abasement.—No injuries could lessen Thy love, O Jesus! There were before Thee those who for years most malignantly hated Thee, those who detested Thee as the most wicked of men, those who ridiculed and mocked Thee in Thy most excruciating torments; still Thy love could not be abated, and no murmur dropped from Thy lips, no vengeance dwelt in Thy heart, but of all Thy enemies there was not one for whose salvation Thou didst not offer Thy blood, so great and generous was Thy love. And how is mine? Alas! It is not a love which deserves the name. An unfriendly look, an unkind word, a trifling offence, suffice to weaken it or to extinguish it entirely.

Contrition.—Then I am without love; I whom Jesus had chosen out of so many thousands to follow Him; I who willingly secluded myself from the whole world and chose Thee for my spouse; I who have meditated daily on Thy example, and after so many years of religious life, after so many graces and heavenly lights, after so many means and occasions to practise love, I am without love.

POINT II.

The Love of Jesus was Wonderful on Account of the Circumstances of His Love.

The first circumstance was the time when Christ prayed for His enemies.

Jesus on the Cross had to speak to His Heavenly Father to commend Him His spirit. He had to speak to his beloved mother, to give her over to the care of His dear disciple, St. John. He had to speak in His extreme thirst to His crucifiers. He spoke to none of these. The first words which He uttered were for his enemies: "Father, forgive them."

The second was that the malice of His enemies continued, notwithstanding His ardent love for them.

Jesus might have waited till His enemies would have acknowledged their guilt and humbly asked pardon. Ah! Jesus would have done so had His love been like yours. I love and I pardon them, said Jesus, while I hear their mockeries; this very moment, while I have to bear their insults, while I actually feel their rage and fury, I pardon them. I offer up My blood for them.

The third was the excuse which Jesus made in His prayers.

The Jews had committed the most horrible crime against Jesus. The miracles which they saw, His innocence, which even Pilate acknowledged, the accusations which they forged, proved their crime. But what were the words of Jesus's prayer? "Father, forgive them, for they know not what they do." As if He said, "O Father, I do not say they have not sinned, but their malice is not so great; it is ignorance on their part; had they known Me, they would never have treated Me thus. Pardon them, therefore, as I pardon them; love them as I love them." How wonderful was this love of Jesus for His enemies! Gaze on Jesus on the Cross, and learn from Him to love as He loved. What was there in His enemies to make Him love them? Human nature, which from childhood is always prone to evil. He, therefore, loved them and had compassion on them. He saw in them a soul He had created to His own image and called to everlasting bliss. He desired, therefore, that this noble creation of His should not be deprived of eternal happiness. In their treatment of Him, He saw the will of His Heavenly Father. For this reason He loved them, and willingly accepted all the sufferings which they inflicted on Him. Lastly, He saw the multitude of sins which He had taken upon Himself, and which the Divine Justice through His enemies was punishing in Him. He loved them, therefore, and offered for them this beautiful prayer.

AFFECTIONS.

Compunction.—I now see, O Jesus, the reason why it has been so difficult for me to love those who have offended me. Had I always regarded them as instruments by which the Divine Justice was punishing my sins, how many acts of perfect love would I have already practised! My heart would now be more like unto Thine, O Jesus! My confusion allows me neither to speak nor to look up to Thee. I confess my guilt, and humbly ask Thy pardon. Alas! O Jesus, I have often meditated on the lofty example of Thy love, I have often admired it, but I have never imitated it.

Resolution and Supplication.—What then shall I do henceforth, O Jesus? Through Thy grace I now have different sentiments. I have again made a different resolution. I have a different will. I shall with all my heart love those who have offended me. I shall meekly and silently bear with their faults. Thus Thou, O Jesus, hast loved, and thus must I also love.

Thou art the only teacher of true love. I entreat Thee, therefore, by the wonderful meekness with which Thou hast pardoned Thy enemies, by the endearing and affectionate prayer which Thou didst offer for them, and by the precious Blood which Thou didst shed for them, to give me a love which embraces all mankind on account of Thee, and to bear all that Thou sendest me through others for my salvation.

END OF THE THIRD WEEK.

The soul is beginning to be prepared for union with God. We have now arrived at the important time on which everything in spiritual life depends. We must come to the determination to follow closely Jesus Christ, and to bear with Him in silence interior dereliction and desolation, bodily sufferings, abuse and calumny, hatred persecution. The one who has not the courage to walk in this way shall never find God, much less arrive at His pure and perfect love. Consider, therefore, attentively the following truths, and resolve at last to walk this road with your crucified Redeemer, and to persevere in it as long as it pleases His Divine Majesty.

First Truth.—The way of suffering is the royal road to sanctity. The end for which the only begotten of the Father came on earth was twofold. The first was, to offer for our sins a sacrifice worthy of the infinite majesty of God. The second was, to be for us the model of the highest sanctity. To gain this two-fold end Jesus chose the way of suffering, which, beginning at the crib in Bethlehem, continued to His last breath on the Cross.

Second Truth.—The way of suffering is most profitable. There are two things which God requires of a soul before admitting it to union with Himself, entire purity of heart, and perfect virtue. The way of suffering is the most suitable for this purpose. Purity of heart is acquired by suffering in a very short time, for in it the soul finds nothing to give it delight save God alone, and the accomplishment of His holy will. It learns, therefore, to withdraw itself by degrees from creatures, to despise all earthly consolations, and centre all its affection on the supreme good; consequently the way of suffering is best adapted to the acquirement of perfect virtue.

Third Truth.—The way of suffering is the safest road to sanctity. Consolations have deceived many; suffering has deceived no one. Souls there were that were favored with heavenly lights and seemed to lead holy lives; but as they were not grounded in humility and other virtues, all these extraordinary graces came to naught. This the "Following of Christ" illustrates: "Some have ruined themselves upon occasion of grace of devotion. They became needy and were left in a wretched condition, who had built themselves a nest in Heaven, to the end that, being thus humbled and impoverished, they might learn not to trust to their own wings, but to hide themselves under Mine" (iii. B., Chap. vii., 2). But those who walk in the way of suffering have nothing of this sort to fear.

Having well pondered on these truths, consider now the exercises of the way of suffering.

First Exercise. To imprint deeply on your soul by frequent meditation certain maxims to encourage you in the time of suffering. These maxims are: I can never suffer as much as I ought for God. I merit by suffering an infinite good. I can never suffer as much as Jesus Christ suffered through love for me. I can never suffer as much as I have deserved for my sins.

Second Exercise. To silently bear the petty adversities which daily occur.

1st. Whenever you have to suffer, reflect on one of the above maxims. 2d. With pure intention offer up what you have to suffer to God. 3d. Speak not of your suffering to any one.

Third Exercise. To offer yourself up to God as a holocaust as long as the suffering lasts. For this purpose be always perfectly resigned to the Divine will; throughout the day renew this act of submission. Patiently await the time which God has ordained for your deliverance. These are the virtues in the practice of which the true imitation of Christ consists. I know you have resolved to acquire them. Offer them yourself to your crucified Lord in the following manner: Joy itself is sorrowful unto death. Innocence itself is pronounced guilty. God hangs on the Cross between two robbers; and all this Thou didst suffer for me; for me the blood streams from Thy sacred wounds; for me Thou didst undergo all the tortures of Thy bitter death. Yet, O Jesus, I do not love Thee. What is the reason of this? I love myself too much; I do not wish to do violence to myself; I cannot bear to suffer. Shall I never die to myself? I have deserved to live in everlasting flames, and I cannot stand the least adversity. I have deserved to live in endless despair, and I cannot endure interior dereliction and aridity. I have deserved to be forever rejected and abhorred by all creatures, and I cannot suffer the least contempt. I have deserved to dwell eternally among reprobates and demons, and I cannot put up with the slightest faults of my neighbor. From this day out I promise to endeavor to resemble Thee, O Jesus! I will henceforth walk boldly in Thy footsteps. Only by dying with Thee can I live with Thee.

THE FOURTH WEEK.

The Unitive Way.

This day comprises the fourth week of the spiritual exercises. On the first day we meditated on our last end and resolved to seek it, cost what it might. To gain this end three things are necessary:

1st. To bewail our sins, extirpate our evil inclinations, and keep our hearts pure and unsullied. This was the first week's task.

2d. To follow Christ and strenuously endeavor to acquire the virtues which His doctrine and example point out. This was the second week's work.

3d. To love suffering and contempt. No one can attain to virtues without overcoming great difficulties and entirely dying to one's self; for this reason we meditated on the sufferings and death of Christ, and resolved to follow Him closely. This was the duty of the third week.

When the soul dies entirely to self, it attains to the perfect love of God, in which our end on earth consists. Consequently, to-day we begin by the meditation on the Resurrection of our Lord; that by considering so great a happiness, we may despise earth and all earthly things, renew the resolutions which we made, and become thereby fit to enter into close friendship and union with God.

EIGHTH DAY.

Meditation 1.

ON THE RESURRECTION OF JESUS CHRIST.

POINT I.

THE HAPPINESS OF HIS RESURRECTION WAS AS GREAT AS THE BITTERNESS OF HIS SUFFERING WAS TERRIBLE.

Christ's sufferings were of four kinds: excruciating pains in His sacred body, extreme sadness in His soul, insults and outrages on His honor, and the inveterate hatred of His enemies. Let us now consider what wonderful happiness arises thence.

1st. Jesus rose with a dazzling beauty of body. To understand this somewhat, reflect on these two points: The glorified body of an elect is of such transcendent beauty that it would enlighten the earth more than the sun in its midday brightness. And were the beauty of all the elect infused into one body, this united beauty would be naught compared to that of Jesus Christ's body. And yet this is the same body which a few days ago was frightfully disfigured, and cruelly maltreated.

2d. Jesus rose with inconceivable joy in His soul. Were the bitterness of His soul's suffering poured into as many hearts as there were on earth, all hearts would have been broken with grief. In like manner should the joy, which His blessed soul felt, be poured into the hearts of all who have ever been on earth, its great sweetness would take away the life of all.

3d. Jesus rose with infinite glory to His honor. Angels descended from Heaven to witness the triumph of His resurrection. Jesus is now their King. He is the joy of the patriarchs, all adore and bless Him as their Redeemer. He is the Judge of the living and the dead, before whom, one day, all the nations of the earth shall appear and either willingly or unwillingly pay homage to His glory. He is the head of the elect; they praise Him forever. Jesus is all this to-day; the Jesus whom Herod derided as a fool; the Jesus whom the soldiers insulted as a mock-king; the Jesus who was nailed on the Cross as a malefactor.

4th. Jesus rose with the fruition of universal love. I say nothing of the love with which on the day of the Resurrection the angelic choirs were inflamed, and nothing of the love of the holy patriarchs. I speak only of the love with which all the elect shall always burn, for they will praise and love Him forever.

AFFECTIONS.

Rejoicing at the Glory of Jesus Christ.—Now the hour of suffering is past, O Jesus, the day of joy has come. Thy sacred body shines more brightly than the sun, and is the delight of Heaven. Thy soul is inebriated with joys. Thy honor is exalted. Thy name magnified in Heaven and on earth. Thou art the centre of the elect which those who are on earth incessantly and ardently seek. I rejoice at this glory and at this happiness. I congratulate Thee on this bliss.

A Desire of the Same Happiness.—Oh, what happiness shall it be for me to rise one day in a similar manner! Who can describe what it is to see Thy most beautiful countenance, O Jesus; to hear from Thy lips words of love; to love Thee and to be loved by Thee, and always to be with Thee? O happy day! I ardently long for thee, O Paradise, and yet how little do I do to obtain thy eternal happiness!

POINT II.

HOLY THOUGHTS AND RESOLUTIONS THAT ARISE FROM THE MEDITATION ON THE RESURRECTION.

First Thought.—As Christ rose gloriously from the dead, so one day you shall rise gloriously if you follow Him. "Know God hath raised up the Lord, and will raise us up also by His power" (1 Cor. vi. 14).

Second Thought.—As Jesus by His Cross and suffering obtained the glory of the Resurrection, so you cannot have a like glory otherwise than by crosses and suffering. This same Apostle likewise teaches, "Be mindful that the Lord Jesus Christ is risen from the dead. A faithful saying: If we be dead with Him, we shall live also with Him; if we suffer, we shall also reign with Him" (2 Tim. ii. 8, 11, 12). What will you think of the afflictions and sorrows of life when this beautiful day shall dawn? O, blessed crosses! will you say, blessed tribulations and blessed contempt that have procured for me this glory!

Third Thought.—The more like to Jesus in suffering you shall be the more like to Him will you be in the resurrection. Hear once more the Apostle: "Knowing that as you are partakers of the sufferings, so shall you also be of the consolation" (2 Cor. i. 7). Mark well these words "as," "so;" they mean, the greater the pains you suffer with Jesus the greater the joys of your resurrection. The more insults and outrages you undergo on earth with Jesus the greater will be the glory of your resurrection. Are not then pains, insults and outrages the most efficacious means to sanctity and the sweet pledge of your future resurrection? And you feel miserable and think yourself unhappy when they befall you. How blind you are! Should you not then raise your hands and eyes to Heaven and thank God? Who are they who despise you and are the cause of your grief and adversity? Are they not those through whom God fulfils His merciful designs; those who make you conformable to your crucified Lord; those who increase your glory in Heaven—in short, are they not your best friends?

AFFECTIONS.

An Act of Faith.—Jesus has risen from the dead. He now enters into His glory, and enjoys in soul and body uninterrupted bliss. This I believe, and moreover if I follow Jesus I shall also rise triumphantly from the dead, enter the heavenly mansions, and live forever in glory. There I shall receive the reward of all my sufferings: for a momentary pain, eternal happiness; for one insult, eternal honor; for a brief moment of sadness, eternal joy.

Compunction.—True it is that God recompenses each humiliation, insult and contempt with a crown of glory. I have forfeited by my pride and vanity many thousands of these crowns. True also that for each interior desolation God bestows a special degree of happiness. How many degrees have I lost by my cowardice and tepidity?

ON THE LOVE OF GOD.

God's infinite goodness towards us, and His infinite goodness in Himself attract us powerfully to the love of Him.

Meditation 2.

God is Infinitely Good towards us.

POINT I.

GOD DESERVES TO BE LOVED ON ACCOUNT OF HIS BEING INFINITELY GOOD TO US HERE ON EARTH.

1st. As God, being eternal, had no beginning, His paternal affection for us had no beginning either, being from all eternity. "Let us, therefore, love God, because God first hath loved us" (1 John iv. 19).

For us He created Heaven and earth; the earth as a dwelling-place for our present transitory life, and Heaven as an abode for our future eternal life. He has loved and has loved us so ardently that for our salvation He shed on the Cross His blood even to the last drop. Throughout eternity there has not been an instant in which He has not thought of us, in which He was not determined to die for us, to make us participate in all His glory and in all His felicity.

2d. Let us call to mind the many graces God has conferred on us. We need only consider the mystery of the Incarnation; it will suffice to prove how liberal God was to us. A servant of a mighty sovereign had stolen from his master a hundred thousand dollars. He was convicted and condemned to prison for life unless some one would reimburse the stolen money. A generous man who had but this precise sum paid the whole amount and set the prisoner free; but by this act of charity he became poor and had to earn his bread by the sweat of his brow. What wonderful love was not this? When, pray, did this happen? Who was the miserable prisoner, and who the merciful deliverer? Let us briefly reflect, and we shall have the answer.

3d. Let us suppose we see Hell opened, and many millions of reprobate souls in the midst of the devouring flames. Christ descends from Heaven and frees one of these damned souls, and reunites it with its body, granting it time for penance. How astonishing would be this act of mercy! This reprobate deserved Hell more than the others. What special love must Jesus have for this soul! This is our own case. Thousands in Hell have committed fewer sins than we; they have not abused as many graces as we; they have not remained tepid as long as we; nevertheless they are lost, and lost forever, and we live and enjoy graces in abundance. May we not say of ourselves what the Jews said when they saw Jesus weeping over Lazarus, "Behold how He loved him" (St. John xi. 36).

AFFECTIONS.

Admiration of the Love of God.—Nothing astonishes me more than Thy love for me, O merciful Redeemer! Thou lovest me and hast loved me with an eternal love. "Yea, I have loved thee with an everlasting love; therefore have I drawn thee, taking pity on thee" (Jer. xxxi. 3). Thou lovest me with an unbounded love, and to what did this love bring Thee? Thou didst become a little child, Thou didst lead a painful life on earth, finally Thou didst die an ignominious death on the Cross. Thou didst love me with a patient love. I have committed a multitude of sins, I have abused so many means, and all this could not lessen Thy love. Thou lovest me yet, and Thou lovest me with a love as tender and affectionate as if I had never offended Thee. I should then love Thee, O Lord, my God, with my whole heart, and with my whole soul, and with my whole strength (Deut. vi. 5). For Thou deservest that I should love Thee with an infinite love, if I could.

Compunction and an Act of Love.—How ungrateful then have I been in not loving Thee, O God, with my whole heart! My Father! My all! I had a liking for any one who rendered me a slight service, and I have not loved Thee who gave me all that I have and all that I am. I was fond of the person who spoke kindly to me and did nothing else, and I have not loved God who died for me. Thou hast conquered me at last, O Jesus! I am thine, exclusively Thine, and Thine forever. I will henceforth love Thee and Thee alone, and love Thee the more ardently the later I begin.

POINT II.

GOD DESERVES TO BE LOVED ON ACCOUNT OF HIS BEING INFINITELY GOOD TO US HEREAFTER.

What does God intend to give us in the next world? Himself. O incomprehensible Goodness! What does this mean?

1st. To possess God means to arrive at the goal of all our desires. As soon as the soul leaves the body, it clearly sees by Divine light that God alone is its sovereign Good and its greatest felicity. From this light arises a vehement longing to enjoy this supreme Good. God satisfies the desire and unites intimately to Himself the soul that has been faithful to Him, so that it is inebriated with unspeakable delights.

2d. To possess God means to see and love God. Throughout eternity the soul shall see in Him new wonders of His Omnipotence, His Goodness, His Beauty, and of all His other perfections; so that it will be ravished and eternally transported with delicious sweetness, and forever feel fresh ecstasies of love.

3d. To possess God means to possess infinite happiness. The happiness we shall enjoy in Heaven is no other than that of God Himself.

We shall taste the very joys, delights, sweetness which God Himself has. How great will be this happiness! One degree of it would be sufficient to make the reprobate forget their present pains.

4th. To possess God means to be loved by God with infinite tenderness. He never regards the soul otherwise than as a child that He loves tenderly; as a vessel of predilection into which He desires to pour out all the treasures of His bounty; as a spouse in whom He takes infinite complacency. As He is infinite Power, which immeasurably surpasses all human power, so He is infinite Love, which infinitely exceeds all endearments of human love.

5th. To possess God means to be happy as long as God is happy. What is the happiness of God? A happiness without end, without interruption, and without diminution. All these attributes your happiness will have. It will be a happiness without end. As long as eternity lasts, so long shall it last. It shall be a happiness without interruption. For as He is infinite Beauty, there will always remain an infinite variety which you have not yet seen; as He is an infinite Goodness, there always remains an infinite ocean into which you have not yet plunged. It shall be eternal happiness without diminution.

AFFECTIONS.

An Act of Love.—My only and sovereign Good, my God, how blind have I been! What can I do to make a return for such astonishing love? Behold me, my God, prostrate before Thee, I offer Thee my heart. I love Thee, and I love Thee with my whole soul, with my whole mind, and with all my strength. I hate and detest all affections and inclinations which are not for Thee. As long as I live I will always prefer Thy honor, Thy will and Thy pleasure to every worldly satisfaction and worldly interest.

Desire to Love God Perfectly.—Should I love Thee as I have resolved, what would be this love compared to Thine! Did I possess all the love of the Elect, I might have something to repay Thy love. O my God and my Lord, have mercy on me! Show forth this hour Thy omnipotent power by completely changing my heart. I ask and desire nothing else but Thy love!

Meditation 3.

GOD IS INFINITELY GOOD IN HIMSELF.

POINT I.

GOD DESERVES TO BE LOVED BECAUSE HE IS THE SUPREME GOOD.

On this foundation the perfect love of God is based. We must love God because He is the sovereign Good, and deserves, on account of

Himself alone, infinite love. What do these words *God is the supreme Good* mean? They mean that God is a Being who has all perfections; a Being who has them in an infinite degree; a Being who possesses and enjoys them of Himself. In order that we may form an idea of God as far as it is possible on earth, we have merely to contemplate a few of these perfections.

Notwithstanding our most vivid representations of God's goodness in Himself, it will be as incomprehensible for us as the course of the stars to a child.

1st. God is Infinite Beauty.

(1.) The Blessed Virgin beholds the beauty of God more than all angels and saints together; and for this reason her glory, joy and happiness are greater than theirs combined. Let us suppose God begins this instant to illuminate her mind, and permits her to see twice as much of His beauty as she has seen until now; the succeeding moment He imparts to her a new light, that she may see twice as much of His beauty as she had seen at the first moment; and God continues so for a thousand years, for a hundred million of years. Will the Blessed Virgin then see the whole beauty of God? No, there will remain of it as much as there is water in all the oceans of the world after one drop has been taken out.

(2.) The number of the angels is many thousand millions, and the least among them has a beauty such that no mortal could behold it without dying of joy. Let us now imagine God to create an angel who unites in himself the beauty of all of them. How dazzling would be his beauty! But still it would be infinitely less than the beauty of God.

2d. God is an Infinite and Almighty Power. All the men who ever were and ever shall be on the earth till the last day amount to many hundred thousand millions. What an immense multitude! On the last day the trumpet of the archangel will sound in the four corners of the earth. "In a twinkling of an eye" the bodies of all departed human beings will arise. The souls that animated these bodies shall return into them, and these many hundred thousand millions shall thus revive at these few words, "Arise, ye dead."

3d. God is Infinite Love.

God's infinite love is proved:

(1.) By His bearing with sinners so patiently. He sees them committing the greatest crimes every day, every hour, every instant, murders of every sort, blasphemies, perjuries, sins that cry to Heaven for vengeance, and sins that bring mortals to the level with or even below brutes. And what does God do? He preserves their lives, and lavishes on them every day new benefits. And as if he stood in need of them, He, by His enlightenment and by His grace is constantly inciting them to "cease to do perversely, and to learn to do well," (Isa. i. 16, 17).

(2.) By receiving sinners so magnanimously.

Let us represent to ourselves a person a hundred years old, who has never thought of God during his whole life, never spoken of Him, but to blaspheme Him, never done anything for God but to offend Him. Can he still have any hope of pardon? Hear and be astonished, ye heavens! This impious wretch in the agony of death says, "O God, infinitely good, I confide in Thy infinite mercy; I am heartily sorry for all my offences, and humbly ask Thy pardon." The pardon shall be instantly granted. "Neither the magnitude of your sin," says St. Cyprian, "the brevity of your remaining term of life, nor the extreme need of your last moments, can exclude you from the friendship of God. His infinite love and compassion embrace all who return to Him."

(3.) By rewarding the just so munificently. Here is this poor miserable human being, who during a whole life has done naught of good, save this single act of true repentance. What reward will God give Him? The possession of Heaven and the vision and enjoyment of His infinite beauty forever and ever. "He shall set him over all that He possesses."

AFFECTIONS.

Confusion and Astonishment.—O my God, Thou art a Good that possesses all perfections in an infinite degree, a Good that deserves to be loved with an infinite love. This I admit, this I believe. How comes it, then, that my heart is cold, insensible and unmoved? I even hate what might infuse into it something akin to love. I acknowledge and see my misery. O Lord God, how long shall I be poor and miserable?

Resolution and Compunction.—I only begin to love Thee when I die perfectly to myself, and to all created things. I therefore now abominate all the sentiments, all the affections, all the words, and all the works of my life which were not for Thee. Thy love shall henceforth be the object of my thoughts, the aim of my desires, and the motive of my works. But, O my God, though this resolution is sincere, I cannot carry it out without Thy strengthening grace. Cast, therefore, Thy merciful eyes on me. Remember that Thou didst create me merely that I might love Thee; remember that Thou didst shed Thy blood for me that I might be inflamed with Thy love. Destroy in my heart everything that opposes this love, and kindle therein its flames.

POINT II.

God Deserves to be Loved, because He is the Only Good.

Neither in Heaven nor on earth, neither in angel nor in man, nor in any created being, does there exist anything which does not proceed from God. Survey the universe and all it contains: the different kinds of trees, fruits, flowers, and plants; the beasts on the earth, the birds in the air, the fishes in the seas. From the earth raise your eyes to Heaven: contemplate the wonders which are there; see the sun whose rays dispense light and heat; the course of the stars, and far above them the everlasting home of the Elect. From these irrational creatures turn to mankind and consider the various gifts with which they are adorned, their diverse qualities, natural and supernatural. Afterwards behold in imagination the angelic spirits and their companions in glory, the Saints. View with wonder their heroic acts, their merits, their sanctity, their glory, their magnificence and their happiness. Then say to yourself:

(1.) Where were these countless millions of the noblest creatures a few thousand years ago? They were all in the abyss of nothingness, and they would have remained there had not God in His infinite bounty and omnipotence drawn them thence. All their beauty, their sanctity, and their goodness is only a ray which issued from the source of all good, God. Thus faith teaches. This we believe, and therefore should be convinced that God deserves to be infinitely loved. Reason tells us this. Whatever is good deserves to be loved in proportion to its goodness. God is an infinite good, therefore He deserves to be infinitely loved. Hence I may infer that if I do not love God with all the powers of my soul, I do not love Him as I ought, and I act contrary to my obligation if I admit an affection which is not for Him, if I perform a work which is not according to His will, and if I do not carry out the designs of His Fatherly providence.

AFFECTIONS.

Confusion.—O my God, I acknowledge and see what Thou deservest, and in what true love consists. A soul that burns with Thy love gives up all attachments to creatures, and tolerates not a single affection which proceeds not from Thee, and goes not back to Thee. It does nothing but what is pleasing to Thee. It suffers everything for Thee, and resists not Thy ordinances. It gives itself entirely up to Thee, and throws itself with loving confidence into the arms of Thy providence.

An Act of Love and Oblation.—I can make amends for all by great and constant fervor. Away then with cowardice! Why can I not do what so many youths in the bloom of their lives, what so many maidens with the extreme delicacy of their age have done? "I can do all things," says St. Paul, "in Him who strengtheneth me" (Phil. iv. 13). This I also say confiding in Thee, O my God, my Strength and my All! Accept then, O Lord, and take to Thyself my entire liberty, my memory, my intellect, and my will, all that I have and own. It is Thyself, O Lord, who hast given all this to me, and I now give it back to Thee; all is Thine own property, dispose of it as Thou pleasest. Give me only Thy love—give me Thy grace—and that is enough for me.

Petition.—Come, therefore, O Holy Ghost! Thou art love itself, and the source of the Divine fire which burns in the Saints. Thou art sanctity itself, and the fountain of all the efficacious graces in souls. Thou drawest their affections to heavenly things. Descend then to-day into my heart, cleanse it from all imperfections and enkindle in it the fire of Thy Divine love. "Compel my rebellious will to Thee." Do me violence, I shall not resist; I ask for Thy love, and to obtain Thy love I am ready to do and to suffer all that Thou willest.

Self-Examination.

Introductory Remarks.

With God's grace, you acknowledge your imperfections, and are displeased with them; you have a sincere desire to die to yourself and to all creatures; you long for union and an intimate familiarity with Him; you desire to experience the effects of perfect love which He grants to those who seek Him with a pure heart. If desires of this sort inflame not your heart, why did you embrace a religious life? Why did you come hither? I came to save my soul, you say. But had you not means for this in the world? If you aim not at perfection, if you strive not for a higher virtue than that of pious people in the world, why did you leave it? But, thanks to the infinite goodness of God, you have other thoughts now, your heart desires true sanctity. I must, therefore, show you the path, and you ought to enter on it, and continue in it faithfully and generously.

For this purpose two things are required.

1st. You must examine your heart, and search into it to find out all your imperfections, all your evil tendencies, till you clearly see in what state your soul is. This must be done during the time which spiritual writers call the Purgative Way.

Prayer to St. Joseph,

To Obtain the Grace of a Happy Death

O St. Joseph, it is not without reason that in preference to other saints we honor thee as the special protector of those who wish for a good death. Thine was so beautiful, so sweet, so precious as to be the envy of all. Thou hadst by thy side Jesus and Mary, ever assisting thee. From time to time they offered thee the relief that their poverty permitted. Jesus fortified thee by the words of eternal life; Mary reanimated thee by the tenderest cares. How many times did not Jesus support with His divine hands thy drooping head! how many times did not the pure hands of Mary wipe the sweat from thy brow! Ah, thou didst die of love when thou didst, in thy agony, behold thyself supported by a God, assisted by the Mother of a God! O holy patriarch, since thy death was so sweet, take, I conjure thee, mine in thy care. Obtain for me, I beseech thee, at that awful moment, a sincere detestation of all the sins of my life; a firm hope in the mercy of my Saviour, who to save me from hell, sacrificed His life on the cross. And, at last, to put my confidence in Mary and thee, I place my soul in thy hands. Abandon me not until thou hast introduced me into the land of the living, where they cease not to bless and praise thee. *Amen.*

your tepidity and carelessness in the practice of virtue, it is hardly possible not to be filled with confusion, not to acknowledge your ingratitude to God, and to feel exceedingly contrite for the many sins of your past life. Hence will spring true detestation of sin, an humble confession and a perfect reconciliation with God. Moreover, at the time of the spiritual exercises there never fails a particular and powerful movement of grace, so that those who do co-operate will eagerly press forward in the way of virtue.

Enter, therefore, seriously into yourself, examine every corner of your soul, with determination such as would be needed to destroy your most implacable enemy. Represent vividly to yourself the state of your soul, and look at it until, through horror, you begin to despise and hate yourself thoroughly.

An examination made superficially produces neither sorrow nor amendment of life; but an earnest and long-continued scrutiny of the soul and its whole load of sins and imperfections is apt to bring on an entire amendment of life.

What I have just said of the importance of self-examination, applies likewise to the manifestation of conscience to Him who directs your soul. There is in the direction of souls no particular on which their progress in virtue more depends. Even the most experienced spiritual director can be deceived if you do not clearly unfold your whole self. Almighty God may, to punish you, deny your adviser the necessary light; on the other hand, when there is holy simplicity and sincerity, heavenly light will hardly be wanting to a spiritual director.

You must, however, carefully avoid falling into a mistake that frequently occurs. Some souls that truly attain to the knowledge of their interior by a retrospective view of their past sins and imperfections, become sad beyond measure, lose confidence in God, grow timid and cowardly, and lastly, fall into a state bordering on despair. They turn thus to their own destruction this only means of amendment. But, thanks be to God, it is never too late, where there is a resolute will. Why? you may ask. Because God is Omnipotent. He can strengthen our weakness, how great soever it may be. He is infinitely good, and refuses His grace to nobody who trusts in Him. He is infinitely merciful, and looks no longer on our former state of life, if we earnestly desire to amend. Thus think of God, guard against the least diffidence in Him; by doing so you will overcome the greatest impediment to your amendment.

True, God gives to the Christian soul the graces necessary to arrive at perfection, but with a certain measure. He prepares for it the fittest means, but in a limited number; He grants life, but only for some time. If all this is let pass by without fruit, then He withdraws from the soul. He may not, perhaps, cast it from Himself forever, but He considers it unworthy of being conducted to union and sanctity. Then darkness ensues in the mind, aridity in the will, a life without consolation, a death troubled with fear and anxiety, lastly pains of Purgatory according to the rigor of His justice. In this retreat, perhaps, your measure of heavenly graces has been filled up; these, perchance, are your last means of arriving at sanctity; it may be these hours of self-consideration are the last of your life. The abuse of grace so long continued should justly terrify you. Waken, then, at once and earnestly employ every moment of the acceptable time. Hear the Apostle: "Whilst we have time let us work good" (Gal. vi. 10).

"Rise thou that sleepest, and arise from the dead, and Christ shall enlighten thee" (Ephes. v. 14).

FIRST DAY.

Examination on Purity of Heart.

The great master of spiritual life, St. Francis de Sales, says: "The first step for those who wish to arrive at purity of heart is to be free not only from mortal but also from venial sin. The second is that not even an inclination to venial sin should remain in their hearts."

We will now examine the various degrees of purity of heart, and then you can see in what degree you are.

The *first degree* is not to commit easily such

venial sins as by their nature lead to mortal ones.

To foster any inordinate affection, when we are conscious that dangerous temptations arise from it, would be a sin of this kind. Not to suppress the first emotion or attack of impure thoughts, to play with them and to be negligent in banishing them, would be a sin of this nature. Another sin of this sort would be to recall to mind vividly some former injury received, and to dwell on it with indignation, when we know from experience that it excites in our soul great anger and hatred. There would be a like sin to give occasion knowingly and willingly to grievous temptations, either by curiosity of the eyes or in any other way.

I call this degree the lowest because these species of venial sin are the most dangerous. We cannot remain long in this degree: either we endeavor to avoid these sins, and thus ascend to a higher degree, or we lose this degree and fall into mortal sin.

They who without remorse commit venial sins, and even boast of them as virtues, have not reached the *second degree*. They tell their confidants all that they have heard of fellow religious, and warn them to be on their guard against them; they persuade others not to be silent on such and such an occasion, but to show their spirit by not allowing such a stretch of authority and the like. This they call true charity. They inspire others with fear, reprehend them, and censoriously impose silence by usurped authority; in acting thus, they look upon themselves as zealous in promoting God's interests and their neighbor's welfare. They speak only of the faults of others, rake up and retail forgotten or new misdeeds, denounce the too great freedom of this or that one, or their love of comfort, and so on. This they call spiritual conversation. Some complain, without remorse, of the Superior's way of acting, criticise their decisions, find fault with this and with that. This they imagine is love of discipline. Others listen willingly to those who detract or calumniate, encourage and increase their slanderous disposition, manifest great sympathy for them, and thus inflame their indignation, and this they pretend is charity.

Souls subject to these faults are either fearfully blind, or terribly malicious. For either they are or are not conscious that they sin. If they are not conscious they are in great blindness, and indeed in such blindness that during their whole life they place a barrier between themselves and Almighty God. If they are conscious of sinning and still persist, then they are terribly malicious, because exteriorly they praise as a virtue what their conscience condemns as a vice.

They who entertain an affection for venial sins have not ascended the *third degree*. There are generally two sorts of these sins. The first is knowingly and willingly to entertain an inordinate inclination for a person or thing, and never truly before God to rid themselves of it, nor to make any serious attempt to banish it entirely from their hearts. The second is, to harbor deliberately a feeling of indignation or aversion for others, to allow no occasion to pass of letting them feel it, and to make little or no effort to divest themselves of such sentiments. As long as a soul adheres to these affections, so long it continues incapable of acquiring virtue even in a moderate degree.

Those souls have not yet reached the *fourth degree* who, although they entertain no inordinate inclination to sinful objects, still keep up certain bad habits of venial sins. Such bad habits are: 1st. To criticise without sufficient cause the conduct of others, and to misinterpret their words and actions. 2d. To introduce into conversation the imperfections of their companions, to make known their secret failings, and to speak of them with contempt. 3d. To murmur and complain about everything and show dissatisfaction. 4th. To backbite and carry tales, and thus create dissension. 5th. To grow impatient in difficulties, and let harsh words escape them. 6th. To be lukewarm in spiritual exercises, and willingly to harbor distractions. 7th. To become sad beyond measure in adverse circumstances, to grow faint-hearted and to lack confidence.

Even pious souls may be subject to some of these faults; we will find very few whose purity of heart is not tarnished by some of these defects. True, in confession they accuse themselves of them over and over; but what is the use? where the amendment? Tell me whence comes the privation of heavenly light at the time of meditation? whence the aridity and insensibility in prayer? whence the difficulty in the exercise of the presence of God? whence the lack of Divine graces, which otherwise flow so copiously into pure hearts? The cause is easily found; one alone of these bad habits is sufficient to draw down upon you these punishments.

Those ascend the *fifth degree* who are at all times disposed to undergo the most painful suffering rather than willingly to offend God by a venial sin, but they do not persevere in this resolution. In truth, some pious souls protest before God their willingness to persevere in their good resolutions; but, their bad inclinations not being entirely subdued, the flow of grace is not so copious and continued as is required for such a high degree of perfection. They often swerve from their course, and hardly a week passes without their offending God venially once or twice. This state is incomparably superior to the fourth degree, but by no means sufficient to experience the effects of pure love.

The *sixth degree* consists in being truly so disposed as to be ready at any moment to suffer the most excruciating torments rather than to offend God by a venial sin, and in being determined to persevere in this resolution. Thus was the holy and seraphic Catharine of Genoa, who often exclaimed, "O my Lord and my God, I would let my body be torn into a thousand pieces, rather than offend Thee by the least sin."

We may know that our soul is in this happy state by two signs. The first sign is for us to pass whole months without our conscience reproaching us with a deliberate venial sin. The second is, if we have committed one, to feel as much sorrow and compunction as if we had been guilty of a heinous crime. The heart which is thus disposed is prepared for union with God.

The *seventh and highest degree is*, not only not to commit a venial sin deliberately, but rarely to fall into venial sin, and then only through inconsideration and frailty. There are only few souls that by continual mortification and by a special grace of God have attained this wonderful purity of heart. They walk the whole day in the presence of God, and no idle thoughts find room in their hearts. They are dead to all inordinate affections, and consequently they are able to repress the first impulses of them. They have a heartfelt charity towards all; they harbor no suspicions, think no evil of their neighbor; they are masters of their tongue, none but edifying words escape from their lips. Thus they walk and cherish in their hearts a purity which we ought to call heavenly rather than earthly.

Such was the soul of the saintly Father Lancicius, who, in his written account of conscience, given by order of his Superior, acknowledged: 1st. That for a great many years no suspicions, no angry or other sinful thoughts had found place in his heart. 2d. That for the space of forty years he never violated the rule of silence. 3d. That for the same number of years he never felt an emotion of an inordinate affection, or a temptation against purity. 4th. That during the space of forty years he never felt a desire of vain honor and esteem. 5th. That for the same length of time he entertained for all men a tender and sincere love, and that he had for his persecutors no feeling of anger, but a sincere love and an ardent desire to do all good to them.

This is indeed a purity worthy of admiration. Here pause and examine again one degree after another. Bear in mind that this self-examen is the most important part of a religious life. All spiritual exercises whatsoever are not sufficient to bring you close to God, unless you reach the last degrees of purity of heart.

SECOND DAY.

One cannot attain to union with God unless the heart be entirely purified; but purity of heart can only be acquired by perfect mortification of all inordinate affections. Even one evil inclination is sufficient to crowd the soul with a multitude of venial sins, and to render it unfit for the love and communion with God. A clear understanding on this important point is requisite for a fair start. Spiritual writers treat this subject at great length, but I will confine myself to those inordinate affections which are the fertile source of others and do great harm to the soul, viz.: inordinate love, desire of esteem and honor, sloth, sadness, anger and false zeal.

EXAMINATION ON INORDINATE LOVE.

According to St. Francis de Sales, love is threefold: natural, supernatural and sinful. Natural love is respect and esteem, even affection for persons because they are blest with extraordinary talent and amiability. This love is neither meritorious nor sinful; it is indifferent unless it be exalted and rendered meritorious by higher motives. Supernatural love is a love of persons in God and for God, because God loves them as His children, and wishes you also to love them. This love is excellent and holy. Sinful love is an inordinate love for persons on account of unworthy motives.

Let us now examine only the last-mentioned kind.

EFFECTS OF INORDINATE LOVE.

First effect.—It alienates the heart from God, attaches it to created things. A soul that knowingly and willingly entertains this love will in a short time undergo a dreadful change. It will feel a vehement inclination for creatures, and equal insensibility towards God and God's interest. It feels happy only in the presence, and is miserable in the absence of its idol. As the conversation with the beloved person is full of pleasure, the Communion with God is replete with disgust. Prayer is interrupted by perverse thoughts, recollection of mind becomes insipid, and we can quickly see that God does not wish to dwell in a heart in which preference is given to creatures.

Second effect.—It contaminates and defiles the heart with innumerable sins. Whoever yields to it opens the door to countless failings. How many sinful thoughts and delights, how many inordinate desires, how many idle words, how much murmuring and backbiting, how many calumnies and feelings of aversion are to be found in those who nourish in their hearts this inordinate love.

Third effect.—It deprives them, in a great measure, of the fruits of holy Communion. True conscience clamors loud enough, upbraiding them for their conduct, and telling them that their life displeases God; but as they love their captivity, they will not free themselves. Whenever they make an Act of Contrition they say it so coldly that they themselves perceive its insufficiency to burst through the chains that bind them. They approach the table of the Lord and bring to their Saviour a heart full of imperfections which causes Him disgust. No wonder, then, that God pours so few graces into such impure vessels.

Fourth effect.—It exposes the soul to the imminent danger of losing the grace of God. To foster an inordinate love in the heart for some time, and not to fall into grievous sin, is just as rare as to carry a serpent in one's bosom and not be bitten. They are on the verge of mortal sin. The reason of this is two-fold: First, inordinate love naturally causes great and dangerous temptations. Secondly, it deprives of the Divine assistance those who seek the danger and remain therein notwithstanding interior inspirations.

MORTIFICATION OF INORDINATE LOVE AND ITS DEGREES.

First degree.—To keep the heart free from all inordinate affection. Spiritual persons ought not to entertain a tender or foolish love for any person, nor have a particular intimacy with any one, nor even occupy their minds by the thought of others; they must have their hearts free and not enslaved, so that nothing may distract them at prayer.

Second degree.—To cherish for another only a supernatural love. This is a high virtue and requires a great recollection of mind. Its practice consists in these two points: 1st. Whenever you converse with a person whom you tenderly love, you must purify this feeling and change this natural love into supernatural by making an Act of perfect Love of God. 2d. Observe the same rule whenever you feel this foolish tenderness for absent persons.

Third degree.—So to purify your love for others that the love of God may not only have the preference, but perfect dominion in your soul. We may love, and even tenderly, but the love of God must always be superior to every other affection. You must, therefore, prefer to have the persons whom you love enemies rather than to break, through love for them, a single rule or be guilty of any imperfection.

Thus St. Augustine and St. Frances de Chantal loved. They both wept and they wept out of tenderness of love; St. Frances for the death of her spiritual father, and St. Augustine for the death of his holy mother Monica. But it is certain that St. Augustine would not have raised St. Monica to life, nor St. Frances her spiritual father, for they clearly knew that their loss was the will of God.

Fourth degree.—In the person whom you love to see nothing and to love nothing but God. A soul that has come to this high degree possesses great heavenly light, by which it sees God in all creatures and in them loves Him alone. If you hold intercourse with persons blest with natural and supernatural graces, you ought to see God in them, how bountifully He pours out His gifts on them; then with your whole heart you should esteem, love and praise in them nothing but God. If others do you any good, you should think that it was God who inspired them with this good wish to benefit you, and that He uses their benevolence to bestow on you this favor. In this way you may see, love and praise God alone in others.

"This is rare," says St. Francis de Sales. "We consider the benefits without thinking of God, or, if we think of Him, we remember at the same time the friend, and so mix him up with God."

Concluding this examination, we can safely say that supernatural love for our neighbor in its entirety is found in very few souls, because there are very few who love God in their neighbor, and their neighbor for God alone.

THIRD DAY.

Examination on the Desire of Esteem and Honor.

We are going to attack an enemy who has subjected to his domineering rule the greater part of mankind. We give over our hearts almost entirely to him, perfectly satisfied to allow him to rule over them with absolute control and in undisturbed peace. To banish thence this deadly foe and to enthrone therein humility is an undertaking in which only a few courageous souls dare to engage. Honor is so enticing for the mind and heart of man as not to be spurned without a great victory over ourselves, and it is not without much ado that we can put aside our senseless notions on this point. All who have not courage enough to do themselves violence, will fruitlessly engage in this combat. What have you done up to this? Has pride been your victor and you its victim?

Signs of the Love of Honor.

First sign.—To have a great esteem of one's self. This is the peculiar effect of this deplorable passion. Religious who are subject to it believe that their talents, their prudence, their way of acting, and their virtues are such that no one can justly find any fault therein. They foolishly imagine that every one should esteem them, they think that they are fit for every office. It is their due and theirs alone. All that is important belongs to them by right. Others in their estimation are devoid of all talents, utterly wanting in prudence, and are thoroughly mean and contemptible. Those who are thus disposed pompously swell with pride, and are in fact an abomination before God.

Second sign.—To love exceedingly and earnestly to seek esteem and honor. All who are thus besotted have an immoderate desire of praise. They wish to be preferred to others, and if it does not happen they become exceedingly sad. They rejoice when others are reprehended and humbled. They are afflicted when others are praised and exalted. They neglect much good and commit much evil to please men.

Third sign.—To fear humiliations, to fly from them, or to bear them reluctantly. The slightest humiliation, how little soever it may be, disturbs proud and ambitious persons. A command or an office which seems to them not honorable enough, a reprimand or censure of their conduct, a look of contempt, the least suspicion under which they fall, a harsh word, a contradiction, a sour countenance, a refusal is enough to trouble them. This is an infallible sign that pride is their master, master of their minds, master of their hearts. Hear what St. Francis de Sales says: " Those who complain of cross words must be very tender indeed, because only words were uttered which died away immediately. I am much displeased when I hear religious say they have been offended by an abusive expression, for there is a great difference between the buzz and the sting of a bee. We must be extremely delicate, and have ears amazingly sensitive if we cannot bear the hum of a fly."

Fourth sign.—To be too much troubled and grieved at contempt and injuries. There are occurrences which are very painful to human nature; as suspicions, false accusations, detractions, public humiliations, abuse and contempt. If religious become sad and afflicted and murmur thereat, it is an evident sign that their corrupt nature is not yet overcome, and that the love of honor is deeply seated in their hearts. The greater their sadness, the greater their trouble and confusion, the deeper are the roots of pride.

MORTIFICATION OF THIS INORDINATE DESIRE AND ITS DEGREES.

First degree.—To contemn all esteem and love of men, and to judge one's self as truly unworthy of honor in the sight of God. An humble soul must infallibly believe that whatever is good in it is entirely the work of Divine mercy; therefore, not to it but to God all praise by right belongs. It must be fully convinced that in itself it is naught but nothingness and sin, and that consequently contempt is its due. " Humility," says St. Francis de Sales, " makes us like poor beggars who think themselves the most contemptible and meanest of all mortals."

Second degree.—To hate all praise and all esteem of men, and if possible fly from it. We should never seek human praise, and when, nevertheless, it is given us, we must interiorly have a real horror of its emptiness. We must always desire the lowest place, and rejoice when others are preferred. We must live to God in secret, and conceal our good works from the eyes of men. " If God, by His grace," says St. Francis de Sales of himself, "has made me fit to practise some works of holiness, and used me as an instrument to do some good, I would wish on the day of judgment, when all the secrets of the heart shall be revealed, no one but God alone to know them, and, on the contrary, all men to know my wickedness."

Third degree.—To bear without trouble false accusations, suspicions, rash judgments, calumnies, abuse and contempt. Those who love humility are not surprised at wrongs done them. They believe they are treated justly, and bear these with calmness and resignation. This is the saying of St. Francis de Sales, "Who is he that sins not, and who in consequence deserves not punishment?" If this punishment is inflicted, let us think that we have offended God, and that it is very just that a creature as an instrument of His justice punishes us. These three degrees are necessary to arrive at union with God.

Fourth degree.—To accept and suffer wrongs with joy. "Oh, how pleasing would afflictions be," says St. Francis de Sales, "if we had truly a desire of salvation! How precious would such occasions be, because they furnish us with the means of practising humility, a virtue so pleasing to God."

FOURTH DAY.

Examination on Sloth and Sadness.

Besides the inordinate love and desire of honor, there are two other evil tendencies which sorely trouble not a few and hinder the whole work of perfection unless they be entirely banished from the soul, viz., sloth and sadness. Truly, the more harmless these two appear the more they injure.

SLOTH.

Sloth is a certain languor and dejection of spirits which are the cause of one either omitting the works necessary to perfection or performing them negligently. From this vice rise many grievous evils. The greatest of them is that the soul in consequence loses all relish for spiritual things, regards the best and holiest resolutions and even sanctity itself as something unattainable by human weakness, and therefore passes all its days in continued tepidity.

SIGNS OF SLOTH.

First sign.—To feel a loathing and disgust for religious exercises. Sloth is for the soul what sickness is for the body. A sick man is not fit for any labor, undertakes it with great difficulty, and cannot continue it through lack of strength. A slothful soul feels thus indisposed. It looks on the hour of prayer as an hour of torment; it begins it reluctantly and cannot keep up its fervor but for a few brief moments, through dryness of heart and distractions of mind, and consequently it anxiously awaits the end. The examen of conscience is neglected altogether or at most is superficial, confession is either insincere or without contrition, and Communion without devotion.

Second sign.—To perform the spiritual exercises without profit. Though slothful religious have gone through them over and over, not a habit of venial sin is corrected, not a single evil inclination weakened. They are as impatient and uncharitable towards others, as obstinate and disobedient to Superiors, as slanderous and as irritable as ever.

Third sign.—Always to make new resolutions and to keep none. This occurs quite frequently. The slothful are constantly forming resolutions to practise humility, but they soon give up the work, and they remain as proud and as little able to bear contumely tranquilly and joyfully as before. Completely tired of the practice of humility, they try the practice of meekness. This they relish no better, when they perceive that they can bear no wrong done by others without evident uneasiness. The perpetual restraint required for the rooting out of bad habits is something too trying for sloth. The consequence of the continued changing is that, after twenty or thirty years' trouble, they have no more virtue than in the beginning.

Fourth sign.—To lead an idle life. Souls subject to this shameful vice have in themselves little spirituality. They live without recollection and without the thought of the presence of God, they hate silence, talk whenever and wherever they can, utterly forgetful of interior progress. In all their employments they are so negligent that they cannot be trusted with anything of importance. St. Francis of Assisi even calls them gnats and flies, because they do nothing else than to hurt and annoy others.

"The kingdom of Heaven," says Christ, "suffereth violence, and the violent"—not the slothful—"bear it away" (St. Matt. xi. 12).

MORTIFICATION OF SLOTH AND ITS DEGREES.

First degree.—To be pleased with the spiritual exercises, and to perform them with great fervor. Prayer is to a religious what water is to the fish. A fish cannot live without water, nor a religious without prayer. Truly religious persons never go to prayer without preparation, are never guilty of voluntary negligence, never shorten the time of meditation; they are indifferent to dryness or consolation, to aridity or devotion. Their fervor is the same at all times and under all circumstances.

Second degree.—To perform these exercises not only with fervor and devotion, but also with advantage to themselves. They who earnestly seek God, seek in prayer neither particular lights nor consolations, but only the amendment of their lives and progress in virtue. When they meditate, they take the resolution to practise on the day such and such a virtue; they also carry out this resolution. When they confess, they direct their intention to some venial sin or other, in order to free themselves entirely from their disorderly affections. They receive for the same purpose. This is to be devout in a practical way.

Third degree.—To persevere in this resolution until the sin ceases. Where there is an earnest will there must be constancy. An example of this is given by St. Francis de Sales, who gradually arrived at such a degree of meekness that every one was astonished. But he spent twenty years in mastering his natural quickness of temper.

Fourth degree.—To lead an interior, recollected and supernatural life. In truly religious persons there can be found no idleness, either interiorly or exteriorly. They perform every work with an actual good intention. They look upon all adversities as appointments of God, and humbly submit to them; they turn all their thoughts on God, and keep themselves in continual recollection.

SADNESS.

Love of God and sadness cannot exist together. Where there is true love of God there is no sadness, there dwells tranquillity, peace and joy in the Holy Ghost. But where there is sadness, there is discontent, loathing and nothing but misery. How could it then be possible that two things so much opposed to one another can be in the soul together? Sadness must either leave it or love cannot arrive at its perfection. We find in the lives of the Saints that they shunned sadness as a ruthless enemy of true love, and by all means endeavored to preserve joy and gladness of heart. Now examine yourself, and see how much you are wanting in this holy joy.

Effects of Sadness.

First effect.—It robs the heart of all comfort and pleasure and fills it with confusion. Those who are subject to melancholy and sadness truly deserve compassion. On a sudden, without any cause, they become gloomy; their memories are filled with a crowd of sad thoughts; their hearts are depressed, even tears gush from their eyes. They listen to no advice; according to their imagination nobody is their real friend, nobody is sincere and candid with them. If any one admonish them to banish these thoughts from their mind as fallacies and illusion, they become angry and more troubled and confused than before, and show thus love for their misfortune.

Second effect.—It deprives the soul of all devotion and communion with God. The thoughts which disturb and confuse the mind draw it ever away from God. The bitterness which depresses the heart, makes an elevation of the spirit to God impossible.

Third effect.—It is the cause of complaints, murmurs and expressions of contempt. Sad people are subject to many inconveniences; they are always full of suspicions and of wild notions. They are extremely sensitive; an unfriendly mien is sufficient to render them morose and sullen for a whole week. Always full of disquietude and uneasiness, there are an annoyance to themselves and to others.

Fourth effect.—It drives the soul into miserable cowardice, and urges it even to want of confidence in God and to despair. This is the last unhappy effect of sadness, that after having deprived man of all earthly happiness and joy, it robs him also of heavenly consolation and confidence in God. St. Frances of Rome once fell into great sadness, and remained therein a long time. Then St. Onuphrius appeared to her and said: "Put away sadness, my daughter; for a soul that is sad is not fit for the spiritual life; if you do not obey me, you shall lose by degrees all fervor and devotion, fall into pusillanimity, and finally into despair."

MORTIFICATION OF SADNESS AND ITS DEGREES.

First degree.—Always to accept all exterior and interior adversities as from the hand of God, and to bear them for His love. Sadness proceeds from our not having true indifference. If, then, we be ready to submit in everything our will to the Divine will, no adversity will ever bring on sadness. The foundation, therefore, on which interior peace and tranquillity rests is indifference about all which God may be pleased to send us. For this there are only two requisites. The first is to believe infallibly that all adversities come from God, that He sends them out of pure love for our greater good, and that He will never desert us if we humbly bow to His holy will. The second is to give one's self entirely to God's guidance, accepting with readiness everything which He metes out to us for soul and body. We must say with St. Francis de Sales, *God knows much better than I how to appoint and ordain all things.* Let us, therefore, allow Him to act with us and to treat us as He Himself deems fit, saying to Him, O God, Thy holy will be done, not mine. Thy law and Thy most holy will be forever pleasing to my heart. "Health and sickness, honor and contempt, life and death are in Thy hands. Give me whatever thou willest, with Thy grace to be indifferent, and I am and ever will be content.

Second degree.—In times of adversity, whether interior or exterior, quickly and vigorously to stifle all sadness. If, however, we unfortunately give way to it, no means are better to rid us of this unwelcome guest than these two: The first is to banish thoughts which trouble and disquiet our hearts, and to be assured that our imagination makes more of trifles than they are worth. The second is to fix our thoughts on God, to adore His most holy will, earnestly resolve to bear the trials He sends us with all submission to His Divine will, and to persevere in this exercise until the mind becomes serene and the heart is entirely at ease.

Third degree.—To submit to these trials with tranquillity and contentment. A truly patient soul is never so far influenced by them as to lose interior peace, and thus to be unable to treat with God freely. It never breaks forth into complaints. It feels the Cross, it is true, but it keeps itself interiorly tranquil, perfectly resigned to the Divine will.

Once an ecclesiastic complained to St. Francis de Sales. The Saint answered: "I have no oil to pour on your wound. I would increase the evil if I treated you leniently. I can do nothing else than to wash it with vinegar and rub it with salt. You say well-tried and wonderful virtue would be required to bear what you suffered without complaint. Your patience cannot be very great, since affliction goes so much to your heart." The clergyman replied, "I have complained only to my bishop, who is my father. Where should a son go when he is sad but to his father?" "O my son," answered the Saint, "how long will you love childishness? Should a pastor of so many spiritual children behave like a child? Do you wish me to feed you with milk like a nurse? instead of the substantial food which grown-up persons require? Are not your teeth sound enough to break and eat the hard bread of affliction?" Such was St. Francis de Sales's answer, and it suffices for the third degree, which is necessary for union with God.

The fourth degree.—To bear all afflictions joyfully. This degree is very high, and can only be climbed by humility, long self-denial and continued exercises of patience, and by the special assistance of Divine grace.

FIFTH DAY.

Two evil inclinations remain to be treated of: anger and inordinate zeal. One cannot sufficiently express how pernicious they are. Since they are opposed to our neighbor, they render our whole life useless, and keep us till death from acquiring perfection.

Examination on Anger.

Those whose temper is hot and fiery have within themselves a strong and powerful enemy, and if they are not constantly on their guard, and do not endeavor strenuously on all occasions to suppress every outburst of anger, they will never be set free from its tyranny. There have been many Saints who by continual self-denial have so tamed and conquered this passion that they were regarded as men of cold and phlegmatic, not of choleric and irascible temperament. We must tread in their footsteps if we desire to arrive at perfection.

Let us see now what power anger has over our hearts.

Signs of Anger.

First sign.—To be excited easily, and to boil with impatience and indignation. There are some persons who are like gunpowder. It ignites when it comes in contact with the smallest particle of fire, bursts into a flame in a moment, and explodes with great violence. A disobliging word, dropped without mature deliberation, a jest uttered without the least intention to offend, is enough to set them all on fire. A refusal or a contradiction is sufficient to fill their hearts with aversion and wrath. They are sometimes even full of indignation without any cause for it.

Second sign.—Through anger and indignation to break forth into impatient words, murmuring and complaints. This is the habit of angry and revengeful persons. If the least injury is done them, they abuse terribly those who have wronged them, and pour out on them their whole venom. They are not satisfied with this, they fill the ears of others with their murmurs and complaints. They imagine this wrong will kill them outright if they bear it in silence.

Third sign.—To continue in anger a long time, and to persevere in it when once excited. There is a great difference between a fire of straw and of large trees. When a fire is kindled among stubble it causes a quick, glaring flame, but soon dies out, while great trees make an enormous fire, spread destruction all around, and continue glowing with intense heat. There are some who are easily excited to anger and make a great bustle, but in a few minutes it is all over; offender and offended are again friends. Others keep up a steady flame, which gleams a long time, harbor a multitude of hostile thoughts, suspicions, rash judgments and contempt, and nourish in their hearts rancor and hatred for whole days, even months.

Fourth sign.—To have a continual hatred and smothered indignation for a person. This is the most mischievous species of anger. This anger arises from supposed or real injury, and is never laid aside. The angry person nourishes aversion in his heart, and will not treat in a friendly way with the persons he dislikes. At all times, and in every cireumstance, he shows little love for them, and still less kindness.

MORTIFICATION OF ANGER AND ITS DEGREES.

First degree.—Not to allow in our hearts a feeling of anger or aversion for anybody, or for any reason whatever. We must have a heart for all human beings, and love them with a sincere love. When, therefore, we feel within us a contrary inclination, we must strive against it with all our might, and never cease until it is rooted out. Let us hear what St. Francis de Sales says on this matter. "We ought to have a charitable and benevolent heart for our neighbor, particularly when he offends us; we have no other motive then to love him than the will of God."

Second degree.—To put down immediately the first motions of anger and aversion. This practice is the only remedy for perfectly overcoming anger and for acquiring meekness. We must, therefore, regard all occasions, which generally excite anger, as special favors of God; overcome ourselves courageously, and endeavor to acquire self-control, self-possession and affability of manners, which are the marks of true sanctity.

"There are some," says St. Francis de Sales, "who are all meekness and mildness as long as everything goes according to their desires; but if any one offends them, they fire up immediately, and like the mountains of which the Psalmist speaks, throw up dense smoke. They are like live coals which lie hidden under ashes. It is no great thing to be kind and charitable towards those who are good; but to be affable and gracious towards those who are perverse, to bestow blessings and favors upon those who persecute us, to speak to those who have attacked our honor in a friendly way, is a sign of great self-denial."

Third degree.—To bear insults with good grace and pleasing looks; not to complain to anybody when we are secretly wronged by suspicions and false accusations. But when in our presence we are offended by fresh abuse, and we suppress our rising anger, and approach those who offend us with affability and kindness, is a far greater work.

Nobody can read without admiration the answer which St. Francis de Sales gave on such an occasion. A rough man attacked him once with violent and abusive words. "Sir, this messenger," said the Saint, "has provoked you to anger; but I will arrange matters to satisfy you fully. Be assured, that if you should deprive me of one eye, I will look on you with the other as kindly as if you were my best friend." Thus acted this great Saint. What do we do? We must sincerely love those who do us evil, and return good for evil. They who love their neighbor only in God and for God, will find in the practice of this degree no great difficulty. Since the motive to love enemies and friends is the same, our hearts, by continual self-denial, can be finally brought to this point, that our love for both be the same. St. Francis de Sales found in this exercise nothing but delight and joy. An intimate friend once said to him, "According to my opinion the precept to love one's enemy is the hardest in the Christian law." "And I," answered the Saint, "do not know how my heart is made; it may be God moulded it differently from that of others; for I find not only no difficulty in the fulfilment of this precept, but rather much pleasure, so that if God had forbidden us to love our enemies, it would be hard for me to obey."

What else can we conclude now, but that all these degrees are necessary, if one desires to arrive at intimate union with God?

SIXTH DAY.

EXAMINATION ON INORDINATE ZEAL.

This zeal is very insidious; it goes about like a wolf in sheep's clothing, which pretends to protect the sheep, but devours them all. It talks of nothing but discipline, of the rules, of virtue and sanctity; but, in reality, it is an enemy of peace, a destroyer of unity, and the cause of innumerable sins. Let us reflect on it more attentively.

SIGNS OF INORDINATE ZEAL.

First sign.—To regard one's own faults as trifling, and to look upon others as momentous. Those who have true love and genuine zeal have always recollected minds, watch closely all the movements of their disorderly affections, remark in themselves the least imperfection or failing; even their virtues appear to them not holy enough. When they are guilty of any unfaithfulness to God, they feel more contrition than sinners of the world for crimes, and punish themselves more severely. If zeal has not these qualities it is not true zeal, but an effect of anger and the offspring of pride.

"O God," cries out St. Francis de Sales, "when will the time come in which patient forbearance with our neighbor strikes deep roots in our hearts?" This is the wisdom of the Saints. Happy those who understand it and act accordingly. We desire that others should bear with our infirmities, which always seem to us worthy of pity; but we exaggerate their faults and deem then unbearable. We watch the faults of others, but are blind to our own. Thus we live and flatter ourselves that we have a heart filled with zeal.

O false zeal, how many eyes thou blindest! Thou growest and becomest grey with years, and goest not away until death! Truly do the words of our Saviour apply to thee, when He says: "Why seest thou the mote that is in thy brother's eye, and seest not the beam in thy own eye? Or how sayest thou to thy brother, 'Let me cast the mote out of thy eye, and behold a beam is in thy own eye! Thou hypocrite, cast out first the beam out of thy own eye, and then shalt thou see to cast out the mote out of thy brother's eye" (St. Matt. vii. 3-5).

Second sign.—To require virtues of a high degree in others whilst we practise none. Oh, how many and great faults are to be found in inordinate zeal! We blame in everything the manners and doings of our Superiors, and yet we require them to love us sincerely, to treat us kindly and to do us all possible good. We criticise every one, and wish to be dealt with mildly ourselves. We attack others with unbridled tongues, and yet we claim for ourselves the greatest forbearance.

Third sign.—To bear neither admonitions nor corrections, and to wish, at the same time, that others be treated with the utmost severity. "We would have others strictly corrected, but are not willing to be corrected ourselves. The great liberty of others displeases us, and yet we would not be denied anything we ask for. We are willing that others should be bound up by laws, and we suffer not ourselves to be restrained by any means" (Foll. of Christ, i. Book, xvi Chap., 3).

Fourth sign.—Under pretext of zeal, to increase the sins and disorders which one intends to remove. Persons who in their ill-regulated zeal try to better everything, are like foolish mechanics, who, in order to fill up an aperture, make many others. What love and meekness cannot reform cannot be reformed at all. Use not, then, severity, and lay not a burden on any one which you would not bear yourself.

Fifth sign.—Inordinate zeal does away with: Reverence and obedience to Superiors, sincere mutual love of religious for one another, regularity in the community life and the spirit of prayer, which makes the cloister an earthly paradise. For what becomes of obedience if everybody is allowed to criticise and to blame the actions of Superiors? Where are love and charity, if every one is permitted to watch, judge, and condemn fellow-religious? Where peace and union, if everybody is authorized to attack others in their absence? Where are the spirit of prayer and recollection, if the mind is full of idle and sinful thoughts, and the heart devoid of true love and compassion?

MORTIFICATION OF INORDINATE ZEAL AND ITS DEGREES.

First degree.—Never knowingly and willingly to think of anything else but of God, His service, and your own soul. All who wish to arrive at interior peace and true recollection of spirit must act as if they had neither eyes to see, nor ears to hear. They must regard all things not committed to their care as not concerning them in the least, and occupy themselves as little with the faults of others as with affairs happening at a distance. Those who do so will, in a short time, experience great tranquillity and peace; but those who do not, lose both time and pains.

Second degree.—To bear the faults of others with patience, until a fit occasion offers to admonish. The Saint of Geneva thus speaks on this subject: "It is not required that you punish an offender on every occasion, for reason and charity demand that you await the proper time until the other is fit to receive the well-meant admonition. A hot and confused zeal throws down more than it builds up. They who desire to accomplish too much all at once do no good, and even soil more that which they wish to cleanse."

Third degree.—To admonish only with meekness and charity, when admonition is useful. St. Francis de Sales speaks thus on the matter: "They who are obliged to watch others and to correct their faults, must first mitigate the severity of the correction in the fire of an ardent love, otherwise the correction would be like unripe fruit for a stomach." If the Saint requires in the Superiors such sweetness and affability, whenever they admonish, how much more will he not require in those who are not strictly obliged to admonish?

Fourth degree.—To make known the faults to the Superior when we believe our admonition is not profitable. As it is difficult for Superiors always to judge prudently and discreetly when, where and how long a fault is to be tolerated, how the admonition or correction is to be given, so it is easy for subjects to fulfil their obligations. If you believe that your admonition is not useful, inform the Superiors, and afterwards keep silence on the matter, leaving everything to od, and praying that He may give light and His charity to both parties.

SEVENTH DAY.

Examination on Our Love for God.

Our sanctity consists in loving God with our whole hearts, and our neighbor as ourselves. Love alone unites us to God. You see, then, what an important subject we have to treat. Consider well the following degrees of this holy love, and examine what and how much is wanting to you:

First degree.—To hate and to shun the least venial sin more than all the evils of this world. There is not a more certain sign of true and perfect love of God than this hatred and avoidance of venial sin. To stay whole months without committing a deliberate venial sin, and if it happens to be committed, to be very sorry and to punish severely in one's self the injury done to God, is essentially the exercise of a soul that is holy and that loves God perfectly.

When the venerable Father Nicholas Lancicius, that master of spiritual life, was told that a certain religious loved God with his whole heart, he asked immediately whether he endeavored to avoid every venial sin. Being answered in the affirmative, he rejoiced exceedingly, and exclaimed, "This is a true love of God."

Second degree.—Not to let a single movement of an inordinate affection rise knowingly and willingly. Nothing is more delicate than perfect love. It cannot suffer the least thing that displeases its Beloved, and consequently it always keeps a watchful eye over all the motions of the heart, and suppresses promptly those which offend God and sully the soul.

Third degree.—To act with great fidelity according to the inspirations of God. It is not possible to love God perfectly and to refuse Him what He, by interior lights, and the movements of grace, demands. God leaves to the foolish and blind dictates of its bad inclinations a soul that does not allow itself to be governed by His holy inspirations. Then it loses the tender devotion it had for God, and deprives itself of all the graces which He had prepared for its advancement.

A saintly woman called Armella, after she had been raised for many years to the most intimate union with God, once held a conversation with one of her friends; when it was somewhat protracted, God admonished her to break it off. She neglected the warning, to her great sorrow.

He immediately withdrew from her His holy presence, and restored it to her only after many tears and austerities.

Fourth degree.—In all our actions to have no other intention than the sole pleasure of God. At the beginning of each important work say, "For Thy love, O my God, and purely for Thee! Thy will be done!" To have this thought so present to the mind that God, who penetrates its inmost recesses, may see that it actually seeks in every word and work solely His pleasure, is the work of a perfect soul that is dead to self and already grounded in pure love.

Fifth degree.—To bear daily adversities in silence and with resignation, and to adore in them the Divine wisdom and goodness. We have to speak now of a very important matter. Imprint it deeply on your mind. God conducts no soul to union with Him until it be well adorned with virtues, and has consequently prepared for Him a fit dwelling. But since virtues cannot be acquired without much exercise, and they are more practised in time of suffering than in an active life, God sends every day some trials to accomplish that design—at one time, contempt and insults, that by them humility may be obtained; at another time, rough and disobliging remarks, that meekness may be practised; sometimes a stern command, that obedience may be tried; at other times disagreeable aud provoking companions, that love of our neighbor may be exhibited, and then, pains, sickness and other interior trials, that resignation to His Divine will may be shown. These are the ways by which God prepares a soul for perfect union. Turn, therefore, in all adversities your eyes away from worldly considerations, and adore in all things the hidden wisdom and goodness of God. This is God's preparation for raising you to the highest degree of love.

Sixth degree.—To desire vehemently union with God. When the soul has fulfilled everything mentioned in the preceding degrees, and faithfully and constantly persevered therein for some time, then the particular effects of grace generally begin to show themselves. Prayer becomes full of heavenly light, and God Himself instructs the soul in the eternal truths. The heart abounds with holy affections. Hours pass like moments. A sweet peace keeps the soul ever tranquil, for every passion is conquered. There especially burns in the heart an ardent desire to love God more perfectly, and to be united to Him more intimately. And this desire increases so much that hardly a mortal here below is able to bear its vehemence.

The pious Armella was so enraptured by this desire that she often seemed to be beside herself. She wandered through the woods, and filled the hills and vales with her sighs and lamentations, exclaiming, "Where is my beloved? Where will I find Him, whom my soul loveth?"

True, in many souls which are in this degree,

this desire is not so vehement, nevertheless it so occupies their minds that they continually think of God.

Seventh degree.—To persevere faithfully when God retires from the soul, and humbly and patiently to bear with the withdrawal of His graces. As long as the soul is not entirely dead to self, the influence of grace and the presence of God do not continue. When God thus withdraws, then all at once every light disappears. Meditation, which before was delightful, becomes an insufferable labor, a painful work, a continual combat, a real martyrdom. The tender devotion, the loving inclination for God ceases; the heart is dried up and insensible. The presence of God, which had for whole days solaced the soul and filled it with the sweetest repose, very often vanishes. Such a soul, therefore, is in a very piteous state. It has no consolation from Heaven, and is not allowed to seek any on earth, in order not to prove unfaithful to its Beloved. But in this dereliction the very thing is obtained which God intended, viz., that the soul may learn to forego all consolation, and place its whole delight in His holy will.

Eighth degree.—To bear humbly the trials of pure love, and remain in them ever faithful to God, however long they may last. If God has chosen a soul which He intends to conduct to the highest degree of perfection, generally He stops not at darkness and dereliction, but sends it greater and severer trials, namely: an uncommon dereliction and disrelish for all spiritual exercises and practices of virtue, a general revolt of the irregular passions, a continual inability to treat with God; then follow grievous temptations, serious attacks against purity and faith, which often last a long time, extreme sadness and pusillanimity of spirit and almost despair. To this are added divers exterior adversities, contempt, persecutions, slanders and so forth. Perhaps you think now that there is not a more miserable state on earth than this? But not so; it is the happiest of all. If God does not lead a soul to union with Himself in this way, a long, a very long time is needed; but otherwise the work is done at once. The violence of the temptation cleanses the soul quickly, and makes the heart so pure that it is very soon fit for the purest friendship with God.

What must a soul do in this state in order to remain faithful to its Beloved?

First.—It must never omit the accustomed prayer. Be assured this time of aridity will not elapse without profit.

Secondly.—It must always continue its mortifications, and refuse nothing to God.

Thirdly.—It must never omit the exercise of the presence of God, be it ever so dry, insipid and seemingly unprofitable.

Fourthly.—It must give itself up wholly to God, submitting to all the dispensations of His providence.

Fifthly.—It must cherish a filial confidence in

God, and, as the more various temptations tend to diminish it, it must hope more strongly that He will never abandon it completely.

Sixthly.—It must not conceal anything from the spiritual director, but must follow his orders with blind obedience. Without this sincerity and submission it is impossible to escape the snares which the enemy lays in this state.

The soul that faithfully endures this trial shall infallibly arrive at union with God.

Ninth degree.—To behold God continually in the centre of the soul, and to be engaged without intermission in the exercise of His love. This is the state which is called union with God. Its secret consists in this: A supernatural light illuminates the understanding, and manifests to the soul the presence of God in such a manner that it remains whole days in the intuition and contemplation of His Sacred Majesty. A supernatural strength moves the will and fills it with a heavenly flame, by which the soul turns itself to God and adheres to Him unceasingly with the most ardent affection. The interior conversation with God, continual though it be, does not hinder in the least the discharge of exterior duties and employments of office. Nobody is more fit for all functions and for all obligations towards God and the neighbor than such a soul.

Wonderful are the annals of the Society of Jesus relating to Father James Alvarez, Provincial of Peru, whose union with God was astonishing in so many important affairs which he had to transact. During twenty-five years he never lost sight of the presence of God.

Tenth degree.—To do always and in all circumstances what is the most perfect and the most agreeable to God. I say *always*. To do so for a few days is something of which an imperfect soul may easily be capable; but to continue faithfully for whole months is an exercise of only a perfect soul which has attained to the summit of Divine love.

Such was St. Joanna Frances's. She undertook no work, either by direction of obedience or the inspiration of the Holy Ghost, which she deemed not the most perfect.

Eleventh degree.—To desire to suffer for God and show the love of crosses and of self-annihilation by accepting all trials as special graces and by bearing them joyfully. When a soul has thus far advanced, it has perfect love of God and enjoys the most intimate union with Him. The love of suffering is the characteristic of the Saints, and the infallible sign of the true lovers of God. This precious gift Christ bestows on those whom He has chosen to experience the highest effects of His love.

Our Lord once appeared to the Blessed Margaret, Duchess of Savoy, and offered her three dishes. On the first was written contempt, on the second sickness, on the third persecutions. The Saint not only was not frightened but even generously said, "Lord, if Thou wilt, give me all three."

Twelfth degree.—To lay aside entirely one's own will and to let the Divine Will be sole mistress. No one arrives at this state unless by singular effects of Divine mercy.

St. Francis de Sales speaking of it says:

"1st. Such a soul lives in an entire forgetfulness of itself, so much so that it awaits whatever God ordains without any solicitude and with a complete indifference. When grievous occurrences press upon it, it turns its thoughts away from them, and sees nothing therein but God alone, praising and blessing His goodness, and letting Him act according to His pleasure.

"2d. Such a soul is entirely dead to self, not attaching itself even to the holiest things, nor wishing for any other exercise of virtue than that which God Himself prescribes."

EIGHTH DAY.

EXAMINATION ON THE LOVE OF OUR NEIGHBOR.

The love of God cannot be separated from the love of our neighbor; one cannot exist without the other. "This two-fold love," says St. Gregory the Great, "is one chain with two links, and one virtue with two exercises." "They are," says another writer, "two flames which rise from one fire, two streams which flow from the same source, two branches which come from the same tree." Therefore, those who wish to know how much love of God they have, need only examine how much love of their neighbor they possess.

Let us, consequently, examine how much of this love we have.

First degree.—Never to offend others in word or deed. As the first degree of the love of God is never to sin against Him, so also the first degree of the love of others is not to offend them.

The practices by which this love will be implanted in our hearts are these:

FIRST PRACTICE.—Never to despise others. Love solely remembers that our neighbors are images and children of God, and on this account it esteems them and banishes all other thoughts.

SECOND PRACTICE.—Never to form a rash judgment of our neighbor. Love, unless when obliged to do so, occupies itself not one moment with the faults of others. It commits all judgment to Him to whom alone judgment belongs. They who observe not this have no regard for perfection.

"Those," says St. Francis de Sales, "who take proper care of the purity of their own consciences form no rash judgments. Only idle people notice nothing in themselves and see everything in others."

THIRD PRACTICE.—Never to misinterpret the doings of others. Any sensible and discreet person never willingly examines the actions of others. One who leads an interior and recollected life never considers the conduct of his neighbor.

"Any work," says St. Francis de Sales, "may have different aspects; it should always be looked at on the best side." We should throw the guilt on the violence of temptation and human infirmity, or on ignorance or thoughtlessness.

FOURTH PRACTICE.—Never to murmur against our neighbors, or to criticise their actions in their absence, or to relate their faults to others. Love is silent in everything, and never speaks except to those whose duty it is to correct.

Second degree.—To have for others sincere and charitable feelings. This is the foundation of true love. We reach it by the following practices:

FIRST PRACTICE.—Not to allow in our hearts any angry feeling or aversion towards any one. "We are not required," says St. Francis de Sales, "to feel tenderly for every one. This is not in our power. Temperaments are too dissimilar. Many are naturally disagreeable. When we have, however, a dislike and antipathy for any one, let us make for this one an act of true love. We must wish persons of this character all good, and be ready to do good to them when and where we can."

SECOND PRACTICE—To rejoice heartily at the welfare of our neighbor. Love has a large and expanded heart; it includes the whole world, and exults at the prosperity of all others no less than at its own. When, therefore, it sees that neighbors prosper it is delighted, feels sincere pleasure, praises and thanks God that He has thus blessed them.

THIRD PRACTICE.—In their trials and adversities, to have a real compassion for them. They who have true love cannot behold others in affliction without feeling sincere and heartfelt sympathy and grief for their sufferings, without praying for them to God, and asking for them grace and assistance. A heart without compassion is a heart without love.

FOURTH PRACTICE—Not to envy others, when they fare better than we. Envy and jealousy are daughters of pride and self-love, but joy and delight at the prosperity of others are signs of humility and holy love.

Third degree.—Not only to live with all in love and harmony, but also to have them maintained throughout as far as it depends on our efforts.

Here follow the practices which may further this degree.

FIRST PRACTICE—To subject our judgment freely to that of others, and to give up one's own will and follow that of another in everything not against the law of God or contrary to the rules. They who wish to live peaceably in a community must observe this, otherwise they will not agree with any one.

There are persons who imagine that they

alone are prudent, that their plans alone are wise, and those of others altogether foolish. If they themselves were Superiors, all would be better in a short time. As long as this self-sufficiency is kept to themselves it creates no disturbance nor disunion; but when it shows itself, it does much harm. I have, say they, more experience; I know matters much better.

"Nothing is more pernicious to human society," says St. Francis de Sales, "than stubborn persons who continually contradict others. They are the pests of communities, the sowers of disunion and discord. They are detested by every one, while the meek and humble are loved by all."

SECOND PRACTICE.—Never to repeat what others have uncharitably said. The Devil uses the talking about others' faults and backbiting as the surest means to destroy union and concord. The world considers it as a friendly act, but, in the eyes of God, it is one of the things which He has a horror of. "Six things there are which the Lord hateth, and the seventh His soul detesteth, and what is the seventh? He that soweth discord among brethren." (Provs. vi. 16).

Fourth degree.—To neglect no opportunity of doing good to others. Love is beneficent, and where there is no beneficence there is no love.

These are the practices of this beneficence:

FIRST PRACTICE.—Never to refuse to do an act of charity when it is asked. This requires lively faith; for faith tells us that whatever good we do our neighbor for God's sake, we do for God Himself. Whoever believes this firmly will never deny another any act of kindness. We would not have had the heart to refuse anything to Christ, while He lived on earth. Believe, then, that whatever service your neighbor asks of you Christ Himself asks.

SECOND PRACTICE.—To seek opportunities to do good to others, and to perform acts of charity joyfully, though unasked.

Love and fire act almost in the same way. Fire extends and consumes all that it reaches. Love does the same; it spreads and benefits everybody it can.

THIRD PRACTICE.—To show sympathy and commiseration for others in times of sickness, by visiting often and by relieving them as much as possible.

Think of the sick as St. Francis de Sales did. "As long as I shall see," he writes to a sick person, "that you are stretched on the bed by this painful sickness, so long shall I feel a particular veneration for you, as for a creature whom God has visited and clothed with His livery. I shall show you extraordinary honor as His chosen spouse. When our Redeemer was on the Cross, He was proclaimed as King even by His enemies. For this reason all souls that are fixed on the Cross with Christ are declared kings. The angels envy us, because we still can suffer, whilst they never suffered for God."

Fifth degree.—To bear silently and meekly with the faults of our neighbor, and to return good for evil.

The practices of this virtue are these:

FIRST PRACTICE.—To put up with all the inconveniences we may meet with in our intercourse with others. For this we need but two particulars.

1st. To show to those who have offended us serenity and affability, and to speak to them as freely as before.

2d. Not to complain of the offence, but rather to bury it in perpetual silence.

SECOND PRACTICE.—To do good to those who have offended us, whenever and wherever we can. This is one of the most perfect exercises which mortals can perform in this life.

The testimony of their consciences, and the inspirations of the Holy Ghost, make them feel then that they have attained the perfection of love.

CONCLUSION.

Virtue is learned by experience alone.

Carry out in practice what you have read, heard or meditated upon; then you really make the *Truths of Salvation* your own. You have hitherto made but small progress in the science of the Saints, because you have practised so little what you have been taught. Follow the example of the Saints, who, by diligently exercising themselves in virtue, obtained a deeper insight into religious truths than learned men could have acquired by years of study.

Indeed an humble husbandman, that serves God, is better than a proud philosopher, who, neglecting himself, considers the course of the heavens (Foll. of Christ, i. Book, ii. Chap., 1).

www.ingramcontent.com/pod-product-compliance
Lightning Source LLC
Chambersburg PA
CBHW021804230426
43669CB00008B/625